英語で学ぶ社会心理学

大坪庸介＋アダム・スミス 著
Yohsuke OHTSUBO + Adam SMITH

LEARNING
SOCIAL PSYCHOLOGY
IN ENGLISH

有斐閣ブックス

はしがき

　大学教育の国際化，グローバル化ということがいわれるようになってずいぶん経ちました。この流れの中で，大学生の留学支援なども拡充されています。留学などを通じて国際的感覚を身につけた人材を社会に送り出すことは，近年の大学の使命のひとつとも考えられています。しかし，大学で教えている立場としては，大学教育の国際化には別の意味もあります。例えば，心理学についていえば，第一級の研究は英語で発表されるので，英語が読めないと最新の研究動向についていくことができません。また，研究者を目指すのであれば自分の研究を英語で発表できるようにならなければなりません。ですから，心理学を専攻する学生には，ぜひ早い段階から英語で心理学を学び，最新の知見に親しんでほしいと思います。

　そこで，筆者（大坪）は2012年から専門の心理学の講義を英語で教えてみました。最初はどれくらい学生が理解してくれるのだろうかと思っていましたが，小テストや期末試験の結果を見ると，日本語で講義をしているときと比べて特に理解度が下がってはいないようでした。実際，日本語の講義であればついつい情報を盛り込みすぎるところを英語であれば本当に必要なところに絞り込んで教えざるをえなかったのがよかったのかもしれません。また，この教科書の元になるような資料を毎回作成して配布し，予習・復習をしてもらったのが功を奏したのかもしれません。

　このようにして，専門の講義を英語化することは可能だと感じましたが，予習・復習用の教科書があったらよいだろうと思っていました。そのときに，本書の共著者であるスミス氏が神戸大学に研究員として来日しました。せっかくなので，スミス氏にネイティブの英語で社会心理学を教えてもらうことにしました。すると，スミス氏も日本人の学生に読みやすい英語の教科書があれば教えやすいのに，と感じたとのことでした。というのも，英語圏で使われている社会心理学の教科書は，内容はとても充実しているのですが，日本人の学生が予習・復習に使うには量が多くなりすぎます。また，英語を母語としている学生には読みやすい，少しくだけた表現も，外国語として堅い英語を学んでいる日本人の学生には壁になります。

　そこで，スミス氏と私は，日本人の大学生が英語で社会心理学を学ぶために，古典的な研究を中心に紹介し（したがって情報過多にならず），くだけた英語表現を減らした教科書を作成しようと考えました。また，すべて英語で書いてあるととっつき

i

にくくなるかもしれないので，本文を読むために参考になる情報を日本語で補うことにしました。そのため，社会心理学のそれぞれの研究トピックを，見開きの左側1ページを英文，右ページを日本語解説という形式で紹介しています。また，社会心理学の実験結果は文章だけではわかりにくいものが多いので，右ページには実験結果をまとめた表や図を掲載することで英文の内容を理解しやすくしています。

本書に含まれる解説と表記について

　右ページの日本語解説は，英語を母語としない日本人の学生，特に社会心理学を英語で学んだ経験がない学生の方を想定して作成したものです。そのため，社会心理学のキーワードだけでなく，社会心理学の論文でしばしば目にする特有の英語表現なども解説しています。具体的には，左ページの英文中で太字やゴシック体などによって強調して示した用語について，右ページで解説しています。本書に含まれる解説とその表記の方針は以下のとおりです。

- 社会心理学のキーワードは本文中で太字またはゴシック体で強調しています。
  - ・太字のキーワードには日本語訳をつけています。
  - ・ゴシック体のキーワードには日本語訳と日本語解説をつけています。

  太字もゴシック体も社会心理学のキーワードに対して用いていますが，ゴシック体にしたものは本文だけでは説明しきれない内容があると考え，日本語の解説を足しています。
- 「心理学論文を読むときに知っておくと便利な英語表現」は太字・網掛けで強調しています。これについては，本マーク（📖）をつけたコーナーで英語表現のルール等を説明しています。
- 上記の強調を加えたもの以外に脚注（英文中では上付きの数字で示しています）をつけた表現があります。これは社会心理学にとってのキーワードではありませんが，日本語での解説があった方がわかりやすいと思われるものにつけています。
- 本文で特に強調していませんが，左ページに収まらなかった情報を「補足」コーナーとして追加している箇所があります。「補足」コーナーの中には日本語で書いたもの，英語で書いたもの，元の論文の英語表現をできるだけそのまま残したものがあります。
- 実験結果を示す図表の中には，図表を読み慣れていない方にはすぐにはデータの見方がわかりにくいものがあります。そのような図には，吹き出しをつけて図

の読み方を解説しています。

本書の構成と使い方

　本書は 11 の CHAPTER（章）からなっていて，それぞれの CHAPTER には 4 つから 5 つの section（節）が含まれています。各 section は見開き 2 ページになっていて，内容もほぼ独立しています（ただし，各 CHAPTER の最初の section には，その CHAPTER で紹介する領域の概要的な内容が含まれています）。自習で本書を使っていただく場合には，タイトルを見て興味をもった section だけを読んでいただいても内容の理解ができるはずです。なお，社会心理学の内容にはお互いに関連し合うものがたくさんありますから，「前の Section ○.○ですでに学んだように……」といった表現が出てくることがあります。そういった部分についても，わざわざ該当する section を読み直さなくても，その section で紹介する研究の概要は理解できると思います。このように，本書は拾い読みもできますし，体系的に学ぼうとするのであれば，それぞれの CHAPTER の section を最初から最後までを読み通すようにしていただければよいと思います。

　余談ですが，上の段落で section という単語を一般的な名詞として使っているときには s が小文字なのに，Section ○.○ と書いているときだけ S が大文字になっていることに気づかれたかもしれません。特定の単語に通し番号をつけて書く場合には，その単語の冒頭の文字を大文字にするのが心理学のルールです。例えば，Study 1（研究 1），Experiment 1（実験 1），Figure 1（図 1），Table 1（表 1）のような使い方があります。上記の 📖 マークの解説では，こういったルールを説明しています。

　いくつかの CHAPTER には Advanced Topic という section を最後に設けています。この教科書では，なるべく古典的な研究（他の社会心理学の教科書でも頻繁に紹介されているような有名な研究）だけを扱い，はじめて英語で社会心理学を学ぶみなさんの負担を軽くするようにしました。しかし，それだけでは少し物足りないと感じられることもあるかもしれませんし，研究領域によっては比較的新しいけれど重要な研究もあります。また，基礎的な内容に加えてぜひ知っておいてほしいというものもあります。そういった内容を通し番号をつけた section と区別して，「発展的なトピック（Advanced Topic）」としました。

　さらに，CHAPTER 10 には Advanced Topic の後に Supplementary Topic をつ

けています。そこで紹介している模擬監獄実験は，社会心理学の実験の中でも特に有名なもので，ぜひ知っておいてほしい内容です（その意味では普通の section として扱ってもよかったものです）。しかし，この実験については途中で研究が打ち切られたという事情もあり，他の社会心理学実験のようにデータが整っていません。そのため，この古典的実験は「おまけ」として扱いました。各 CHAPTER で section として通し番号をつけているものに加えて，Advanced Topic（および Supplementary Topic）として紹介している内容にもぜひ挑戦してみてください。

　冒頭でも述べたように，本書は社会心理学の教育を英語化することを目的として執筆しました。この目的自体は現在の大学教育改革の流れにも対応していて，特に奇をてらったものではないと思います。しかし，本書のように英語で社会心理学を学ぶ・教えるという目的に特化した教科書はこれまで出版されておらず，このような教科書にいったいどれくらい需要があるのかわかりませんでした。そんな中，2016 年度の社会心理学会において，出版前の本書の原稿を紹介するワークショップの機会を与えていただいたこと，そして多くの先生にそのワークショップに参加していただいたことにはずいぶん勇気づけられました。ワークショップの機会を与えていただいた三浦麻子先生（関西学院大学）には記して感謝申し上げます。また，需要の読めない教科書を出版することを決定し背中を押していただいた有斐閣にも感謝しています。特に書籍編集第 2 部の中村さやかさんには，英語で社会心理学を学んだことがない学生の視点で，本書の内容をわかりやすいものにするための多くのコメントをいただきました。学生のみなさんにとって本書が読みやすいものになっているとすれば，中村さんのアドバイスに多くを負っています。

　本書の目的である社会心理学教育の英語化の先には，学生のみなさんが第一線の研究論文を自分自身で読むことができるようになること，さらに研究者を目指す方が英語で研究発表できるようになることがあります。本書がこのような広い意味で社会心理学の国際化に貢献できれば，筆者にとっても望外の喜びです。

2017 年 11 月

著者を代表して　大坪　庸介

本書をお使いになる先生方へ

　本書を授業で使っていただく場合，英語パートの全訳があると便利だと感じられることがあるかもしれません。例えば，演習形式の授業で使っていただく場合には，事前に学生に英文を読ませた上で日本語訳を与えて復習してもらうという使い方もあるかもしれません。そのため，筆者の研究室の大学院生である山口真奈氏に日本語訳を作成してもらいました。山口氏はカリフォルニア大学ロサンゼルス校を心理学専攻（人類学副専攻）で卒業しており，本書の翻訳には適任でした。

　本書を大学等の授業・ゼミ等にてテキストとして採用いただく先生方で，上記の日本語訳データをご希望の方は，以下のメールアドレス（有斐閣書籍編集第2部）までご連絡ください。

　　お申し込みメールアドレス　sho2@yuhikaku.co.jp

　※件名を「『英語で学ぶ社会心理学』日本語訳データ希望」としていただき，メール内に
　　・お名前
　　・ご所属（学生の方は不可）
　　・資料送付先のメールアドレス（ハードコピーをご希望の方は送付先ご住所）
　　・ご採用予定の授業名
　を明記の上，お申し込みください。

著者紹介

大坪 庸介（おおつぼ ようすけ）

現在　東京大学大学院人文社会系研究科教授

主著　『仲直りの理――進化心理学から見た機能とメカニズム』ちとせプレス（2021）.
『進化でわかる人間行動の事典』朝倉書店（2021）.（共編）
『進化と感情から解き明かす社会心理学』有斐閣（2012）.（共著）

Adam Smith（アダム・スミス）

現在　国際基督教大学教育学部アーツ・サイエンス学科助教

主著　"Perceived goal instrumentality is associated with forgiveness: A test of the valuable relationships hypothesis." *Evolution and Human Behavior. 41*, 58-65.（2020）.（共著）
"Cooperation: The roles of interpersonal value and gratitude." *Evolution and Human Behavior, 38*, 695-703.（2017）.（共著）

【日本語訳（テキスト採用者用資料）作成者】

山口 真奈（やまぐち まな）

2022年3月　神戸大学大学院人文学研究科博士課程後期課程修了（学術博士）

主著　"Loneliness predicts insensitivity to partner commitment." *Personality and Individual Differences, 105*, 200-207.（2017）.（共著）
"Commitment signals in friendship and romantic relationships." *Evolution and Human Behavior, 36*, 467-474.（2015）.（共著）
"Experiential purchases and prosocial spending promote happiness by enhancing social relationships." *Journal of Positive Psychology, 11*, 480-488.（2016）.（共著）

目　次

はしがき i
本書をお使いになる先生方へ v
著者紹介 vi

CHAPTER 1　Introduction to Social Psychology
社会心理学とは　　1

1.1	What is Social Psychology?	2
1.2	Situational Influence: An Illustrative Study	4
1.3	Social Psychological Experiments Ⅰ: Theory	6
1.4	Social Psychological Experiments Ⅱ: Control	8
1.5	Why Not Use Introspection?	10
Advanced Topic	The Person-Situation Interaction	12

CHAPTER 2　Self
自己　　15

2.1	What is the Self?	16
2.2	Self-Schema: The Cognitive Structure of Self	18
2.3	Positive Illusions and Mental Health	20
2.4	Social Comparison and Self-Evaluation	22
2.5	Self-Esteem Tracks Others' Valuation of the Self	24
Advanced Topic	Self-Regulation and Delay of Gratification	26

vii

Social Cognition

社会的認知 29

3.1	How Well Do Our Thoughts Reflect Reality?	30
3.2	Errors in Causal Attributions	32
3.3	Prior Knowledge Influences Perception	34
3.4	Illusory Correlation	36
3.5	Heuristics and Cognitive Biases	38
Advanced Topic	The Accuracy of Social Cognition	40

Impression Formation and Interpersonal Attraction

印象形成と対人魅力 43

4.1	Forming Impressions of Others	44
4.2	"Diagnosticity" of Social Information	46
4.3	Proximity and the Mere Exposure Effect	48
4.4	Do Birds of a Feather Really Flock Together?	50
4.5	The Effect of Physical Attractiveness	52

Emotions

感情・情動 55

5.1	Affect, Emotion, and Mood	56
5.2	The Role of Bodily Feedback: The James-Lange Theory	58
5.3	The Role of Interpretation: The Two-Factor Theory	60
5.4	Do Emotions Require Cognition?	62
5.5	Basic Emotions and Facial Expressions	64

Attitudes and Persuasion
態度と説得　67

6.1	Do Attitudes Predict Behavior?	68
6.2	What is the Causal Direction of the Attitude-Behavior Relationship? Cognitive Dissonance Theory	70
6.3	Persuasion Techniques	72
6.4	Dual Routes to Persuasion	74
Advanced Topic	How to Measure Socially Undesirable Attitudes: The Implicit Association Test	76

Social Influence
社会的影響　79

7.1	The Influence of Social Settings: Social Facilitation	80
7.2	Social Loafing	82
7.3	Conformity to the Majority Ⅰ	84
7.4	Conformity to the Majority Ⅱ	86
7.5	Minority Influence	88
Advanced Topic	Social Exclusion Hurts	90

Intergroup Relations
集団間関係　93

8.1	The Power of Intergroup Situations	94
8.2	The Robbers Cave Experiment	96
8.3	Social Identity Theory	98
8.4	Cognition in Intergroup Contexts	100
8.5	Intergroup Contact Reduces Prejudice	102
Advanced Topic	Are There Hidden Forms of Racism?	104

目　次　ix

Prosocial Behavior

向社会的行動　107

9.1	Situational Influence on Prosocial Behavior	108
9.2	The Empathy-Altruism Hypothesis	110
9.3	The Murder of Kitty Genovese and Unresponsive Bystanders	112
9.4	The Bystander Effect and Diffusion of Responsibility	114
Advanced Topic	Punishment and Cooperation	116

Antisocial Behavior

反社会的行動　119

10.1	Aggressive Behavior	120
10.2	Aggression Can Be Socially Learned	122
10.3	Obedience to Authority I	124
10.4	Obedience to Authority II	126
Advanced Topic	Long-term Effects of Media Violence	128
Supplementary Topic	The Stanford Prison Experiment	130

Cultural Psychology

文化心理学　133

11.1	How Does Culture Affect the Social Mind?	134
11.2	Self and Other in the Context of East and West	136
11.3	Holistic versus Analytic Thought	138
11.4	Choice and Motivation in the Context of East and West	140
Advanced Topic	Self and Motivation	142

索　引 ………………………………………………… 145

📖 心理学論文を読むときに知っておくと便利な英語表現

"i.e." と "e.g."　3

著者が3人以上の場合に使う "et al."　5

一般的ではない複数形をとる単語　7

1997a, 1997b　11

引用文献の表記法　14

〜 not の短縮形　17

引用の決まり　21

引用以外でのクォーテーション・マーク（" "）の使い方　23

実験デザインの表記法　25

Term paper　27

See ... for a review　27

Scholastic Aptitude Test (SAT)　27

実験の本当の目的を隠しているときの表現　31

Significant：有意な　31

Systematic：系統的な　31

Essay　33

It is 〜, That is 〜の短縮形　35

実験のデザイン（要因計画）について　47

Unconsciousness：無意識または非意識　49

Eponymous　59

Chance level　65

Anecdote　75

Unanimity：全員一致　85

Naive participants　89

Doubt と suspect　129

著者のイニシャル　135

本書のコピー，スキャン，デジタル化等の無断複製は著作権法上での例外を除き禁じられています。本書を代行業者等の第三者に依頼してスキャンやデジタル化することは，たとえ個人や家庭内での利用でも著作権法違反です。

CHAPTER 1

Introduction to Social Psychology
社会心理学とは

1.1
What is Social Psychology?

1.2
Situational Influence: An Illustrative Study

1.3
Social Psychological Experiments Ⅰ: Theory

1.4
Social Psychological Experiments Ⅱ: Control

1.5
Why Not Use Introspection?

Advanced Topic
The Person-Situation Interaction

1.1 What is Social Psychology?

The primary goal of **social psychology** is to understand *how people think, feel, and act in social situations*. As social psychologists have long known, the presence of others, be they real or imagined, has a powerful influence on human psychology. For example, suppose you can play Beethoven's Moonlight Sonata very well, at least when you are alone. How well do you think you can play it when you are not alone, when you are on stage in front of a large audience? It is quite likely that your performance would be influenced by the presence of the audience, even though they only quietly listen from their seats. You may become anxious and notice that a certain part of the sonata is more difficult than usual. Or by contrast, you may find the audience to be a source of vigor, and perform more passionately than ever (we will see which outcome is more likely under what conditions in CHAPTER 7). Either way, the presence of others can change our **cognitions** (how we think), **emotions** (how we feel), and **behavior** (how we act).

After a short introduction (CHAPTER 1), this textbook aims to acquaint you with "the classics" of social psychology, the well-known studies that deal with cognitions, emotions, and/or behaviors in the context of social settings. We first explore the social nature of the self (CHAPTER 2), after which we examine how our thoughts are shaped by social settings as well as how we think about other people (CHAPTERs 3 & 4). We next investigate emotions (CHAPTER 5) and attitudes (CHAPTER 6). Continuing our journey, we consider how cognitions, emotions, and behaviors are influenced in general by the presence of others (CHAPTER 7) and in specific by outgroup members (CHAPTER 8). Towards the end (CHAPTERs 9 & 10), we look at two distinct types of social behavior—prosocial behaviors (**i.e.**, behaviors complying with social norms) and antisocial behaviors (**e.g.**, aggression). Finally, we explore how the social mind is influenced by culture (CHAPTER 11).

Throughout this textbook, we include as many examples of social psychological experiments as possible. In studying these examples, you are likely to find that social psychological explanations differ from the kinds of explanations you are used to hearing in daily life. This is because people typically assume that personal factors (personality and other individual differences), as opposed to **situational** (or **external**) **factors**, are the best way to explain the actions of others. For example, if someone performed the Moonlight Sonata terribly while on stage, one may rush to conclude that he/she is a poor pianist, without considering the importance of situational factors (e.g., how the presence of the audience affects performance). However, as we will see in this introductory chapter, there is a good underlying reason for using the experiment as a research tool—situational factors, as compared to personal factors, are often better predictors of why we think, feel, and act in the various ways that we do.

社会心理学（Social Psychology）の研究対象——Cognition は認知，emotion は感情（または**情動**），behavior は行動と訳します。

　この3つ組が社会心理学にとって大事なのは，心のはたらき（認知と感情）と，そのはたらきの結果として外に現れるもの（行動）からなっていて，心理学の関心内容を尽くしているためです。

　したがって，社会心理学とは心理学で大事な3つ組と他者の存在（presence of others）との関係を調べていく領域です。本文の中で"be they real or imagined"（他者〔others〕が実際の他者であれ想像上の他者であれ）と書いているのは，私たちは，その場に誰もいなくても，「あの人がいたらどう思うだろうか」というように，誰か架空の他者の存在を想定して，その架空の他者に3つ組が影響を受けることがあるからです（感情と情動の区別については，Section 5.1 を参照）。

📖 **"i.e."と"e.g."**　　i.e. は that is（すなわち）という意味です。e.g. は for example（例えば）の意味です。どちらもラテン語の省略（i.e. は id est，e.g. は exempli gratia）なので英語表現の頭文字をとったものにはなっていません。
　左ページでは i.e. や e.g. の後にコンマ（,）がついています。これは，that is, ... や for example, ... のように，省略しない表現のときにコンマをつけているのと同じです。また，ピリオドまで含めて省略形なので，勝手に ie や eg にしてはいけません。
　日本語で「例えば」を ex と記載することがありますが，ex は example の省略形で，for example（例えば）の意味としては英語では用いません。注意しましょう。

社会的状況の力　　社会心理学は，私たちがどのように感じ，考え，行動するかを予測する際に，その人がどのような人物かということよりも，その人がどのような状況にいるかを重視します。つまり，社会心理学とは**状況要因**（**situational factor**）または**外的要因**（**external factor**）が大事だと考える学問です。

　心理学の中には，「その人がどのような人か」を重視する分野もあります。その代表はパーソナリティ心理学（personality psychology）です。

1.2 Situational Influence: An Illustrative Study

Imagine that you witness someone throw an empty can on the street. It is likely you will think the person has an antisocial **disposition**. However, some scholars have a different explanation. Consider the **Broken Window Theory**. According to this theory, "signs of disorder like broken windows, litter, and graffiti induce other (types of) disorder and petty crime" (Keizer, Lindenberg, & Steg, 2008, p. 1681). Notice this theory assumes that antisocial behavior is caused by situational factors, such as broken windows, litter, and graffiti. An unstated assumption of the theory is that the same person behaves differently when signs of disorder are present compared to when they are not.

A team of Dutch researchers experimentally examined the Broken Window Theory (Keizer et al., 2008). The specific **hypothesis** they tested was that the presence of graffiti causes littering. Making use of an alley that was commonly used to park bicycles, Keizer et al. conducted an experiment over the course of two days. During the night before the first day of the experiment, the researchers painted the main wall of the alley, removing all signs of dirtiness and graffiti. The researchers called this the "order condition" because there were no cues of disorder. During the night before the second day of the experiment, the researchers painted some graffiti on the wall, thereby creating the "disorder condition." The experimental settings of the two conditions are shown in Figure 1-1. Note that in both conditions there is a highly visible sign prohibiting graffiti. Therefore, people could easily discern that a social norm (i.e., no graffiti) was violated (i.e., the wall was covered in graffiti) in the disorder condition.

Each day, after the alley became filled with bicycles, the researchers attached a commercial flyer to the bicycles' handlebars. Then, the researchers simply observed what each cyclist did with the flyer when he or she came to pick up their bicycle. The researchers "counted throwing the flyer on the ground or hanging it on another bicycle as littering" (Keizer et al., 2008, p. 1683). "Not-littering" involved "taking the flyer with them" because there was no trash can around the area.

The results of this experiment are depicted in Figure 1-2. While only 33% of cyclists littered in the absence of graffiti, when graffiti was on the wall, 69% of cyclists littered. This result clearly demonstrates the power of situational influence: The situational factor (i.e., the presence of graffiti on the wall) made people twice as likely to behave in an antisocial manner!

Figure 1-1. Experimental setting used in Keizer et al.'s study. (a) The order condition. (b) The disorder condition. [Keizer et al., 2008]

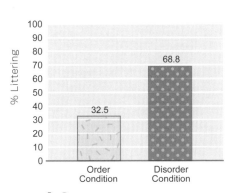

Figure 1-2. Percentage of cyclists who littered as a function of experimental condition (Order vs. Disorder). [Keizer et al., 2008 より筆者作成]

英語で「条件ごとの」というときには，上記の as a function of という表現を使います。

Disposition：傾性　ある人の行動傾向（例えば，反社会的行動をしやすい）のことです。行動を規定する個人要因（personal factor）とほぼ同義です。

Broken Window Theory：割れ窓理論

📖 著者が3人以上の場合に使う"**et al.**"　ラテン語の et alii からきた言葉で，and others という意味です。論文を引用するときに，3人以上の著者によって書かれた論文は，最初は Keizer, Lindenberg, & Steg のように全員の名前を書きますが，2回目以降は最初の1人の名前とその他という意味で，Keizer et al. のように書きます。この et al. は，al の後のピリオドまで含めて正式な表記方法です。ここでのピリオドは，「本来もっと長い単語（alii）を省略しましたよ」ということを意味しています。ただし，著者が6人以上いる場合には，全員の名前を書くと長くなるので，最初から et al. を使って省略して書きます（これはアメリカ心理学会のルールです）。

Hypothesis：仮説　「仮説が証明された」という表現をする人がときどきいますが，心理学では「証明された」という表現は用いません。一般的には「仮説が支持された（the hypothesis was supported）」を使います。また，英語では confirmed（正しさが確認された）も使われます。

1.3 Social Psychological Experiments I : Theory

Experiments act to test particular **hypotheses**, but hypotheses do not appear out of thin air; they are derived from **theories** that specify relationships among **constructs**. Common constructs (i.e., abstract concepts and ideas) studied by psychologists include attractiveness, attitudes, cooperation, antisocial behavior, and so on.

In the Broken Window Theory, the two main constructs are signs of disorder and antisocial behavior. Signs of disorder refer to any noticeable thing that indicates someone has committed antisocial behavior. For example, a broken window suggests that someone engaged in vandalism, while graffiti indicates that someone painted on a surface they do not own. Antisocial behavior is almost any kind of *bad* behavior, and includes a wide variety of acts that are destructive to society. These acts may violate laws (in which case they are illegal) or social norms, implicit rules that are generally agreed upon (e.g., don't cut in front of someone who is waiting in line at the grocery store).

Psychological theories typically attempt to explain **causal relationships** among constructs. Relationships such as "A causes B" or "smoking causes cancer" are instances of causal relationships. In a similar manner, the core idea of the Broken Window Theory can be paraphrased as "signs of disorder cause antisocial behavior."

Theories are typically too abstract to test directly. Therefore, researchers derive testable hypotheses from their theories. In Keizer et al.'s (2008) experiment, the hypothesis was that "the presence of graffiti on the wall would cause littering." In deriving this hypothesis, Keizer et al. assumed that people would perceive graffiti as a sign of disorder. They also assumed that littering was an instance of antisocial behavior. Such assumptions are called **operational definitions**, which are links between abstract constructs and observable or measurable objects. Although it is difficult to determine whether a sign of disorder is present in a setting (because what counts as a sign of disorder is somewhat ambiguous), it is easy to determine whether graffiti is present or not, in a particular setting.

You may wonder whether only one experiment employing a particular set of operational definitions is sufficient to verify a theory. This is a really good question. Researchers usually do not consider the results of only one experiment to be conclusive. To confirm the validity of the Broken Window Theory, Keizer et al., in fact, reported on six different experiments whereby various operational definitions of signs of disorder (e.g., a bunch of shopping carts strewn about a parking lot) and resultant antisocial behavior (e.g., the likelihood of taking versus returning some found money) were studied. Thus, to the degree that different studies with different operational definitions consistently support the same theory, we can be more confident about the validity of that theory.

📖 **一般的ではない複数形をとる単語**　網がかかっている **hypotheses** の語尾に注目してください。和英辞書で「仮説」と引くと hypothesis となっています。語尾は"sis"になっています。語尾が"ses"となっているのは，この hypothesis の複数形です。この一文字の違いで，著者が複数の仮説について議論しているのか，ひとつの仮説について議論しているのかが違ってくるので気をつけてください。

　この他に実験の刺激という意味でよく使われる stimulus の複数形は stimuli になります。指標の意味で使われる index には indexes 以外に indices という複数形があります。

Theory：理論

Construct：構成概念

Causal Relationship：因果関係　　Causal relationship は correlation（相関関係）と区別されます。correlation は A と B の間に一方が大きな値をとれば他方も大きな値をとる（または，一方が大きな値をとれば他方は小さな値をとる）という関係があることを意味します（A が B の原因となっているわけではありません）。例えば，兄弟の身長には相関がありますが（お兄ちゃんの背が高ければ弟も背が高い），お兄ちゃんの身長が弟の身長の原因となっているわけではありません。

　また，調査の結果，子どもが家庭で暴力的な番組を視聴しているほど学校での暴力的傾向が高いという関係が見られたとします。私たちはつい暴力的な番組の視聴が子どもを暴力的にするという因果関係を想定しがちですが，この調査結果からわかるのは相関関係があったということだけです（例えば，暴力的傾向が高いから暴力的な番組を見たがるという場合も同じ結果が得られます）。本当に因果関係があるのかどうかはもっと厳密に調べてみる必要があります（この問題に興味のある方は，CHAPTER 10 の Advanced Topic を参照してください）。

Operational Definition：操作的定義

1.4 Social Psychological Experiments II: Control

Experiments are an ideal research method to test causal hypotheses. Suppose you observed that littering is more common in places where graffiti is present than in places where graffiti is absent. This observation is not direct evidence for the Broken Window Theory. The observed pattern might be due to the fact that a variety of antisocial behaviors (including both graffiti and littering) are more common in places where many unemployed people live or in neighborhoods with high levels of gang violence; or perhaps the presence of graffiti simply causes people to notice litter more often than when graffiti is absent. The possible explanations are endless. Experiments are free from such ambiguous explanations because researchers manipulate causal elements.

In Keizer et al.'s (2008) experiment, the researchers had full **control** over the experimental setting. "Control" means the researchers changed only the variable of interest (in this case, the cue of disorder), while keeping all other things as equal as possible. Such experimental control allows the researchers to test a hypothesized causal relationship: Because only the presence of graffiti differed in the two conditions, the researchers can conclude that the difference in the percentage of people who littered was caused by the presence/absence of graffiti.

Psychologists call the causal part of their hypotheses an **independent variable**. The term "variable" is used because it takes on different values. In Keizer et al.'s experiment, the independent variable took on two different values: Graffiti was present or not (1 or 0). The term "independent" is used because it connotes freedom; researchers can *freely* determine the value of the independent variable. By spray painting graffiti on one day and removing it on the other, Keizer et al. manipulated the experimental setting as they wanted. Based on this **manipulation**, the researchers created two situations: in one situation the cue of disorder was present, in the other it was not. Because Keizer et al. conducted their study outside the laboratory (as a **"field experiment"**), they could not control who participated in their study. However, if you run an experiment in a laboratory, you have full control over which **participant** is assigned to which condition. Ideally, research participants are randomly assigned to different experimental conditions. This standard is called **random assignment**.

The measure of the final outcome is called the **dependent variable**. Its value (e.g., littering or not) depends on each person who is observed, and thus the experimenter cannot freely determine the value. Moreover, what value it will take is supposed to depend on the value of the independent variable. Based on the hypothesis derived from the Broken Window Theory, when graffiti is present, we anticipate that littering will be more likely than when graffiti is absent.

Control：統制　　自分が関心のある変数以外の要因の効果を「統制する」という意味です。例えば，割れ窓理論の実験では，実験を実施する曜日，時間帯，天気などを2つの条件で同じにすることで，ポイ捨てに影響しそうな他の要因の効果を2つの条件で一定に保つことができると考えられます。

　このように，他の要因の効果を一定に保ちつつ，実験条件から自分が関心のある変数だけを取り除いた条件を control condition（統制条件）といいます。割れ窓理論の実験では，自転車置き場のその他の状況がまったく同じなのに，無秩序の手がかり（落書き）だけがない条件のことです。

Independent Variable／Dependent Variable：独立変数／従属変数　　日本語で独立変数と従属変数と書くと，なぜここで支配関係のような言葉が出てくるのかと思われるかもしれません。

　実は，これは英語での表現のニュアンスを伝える訳語が日本語にないのが問題です。例えば，「人々はポイ捨てをしがちかどうか？」と聞かれたとしましょう。皆さんはすでに壁に落書きがあるとか，無秩序を示す手がかりがあるかどうかが大事だということを知っています。そこで「それは状況次第だ」と答えるかもしれません。英語では，この「それは状況次第だ」を"it depends"というのです。

　つまり，dependent variable とは状況次第で値が変わってしまう変数ということです。それに対して，状況まかせにするのではなく実験者が操作するほうを independent variable（状況次第ではない変数）と覚えるとよいでしょう。

Manipulation：操作

Field Experiment：フィールド実験

Participant：（実験）参加者　　以前は subject（被験者）と呼んでいて，古い論文では subject という表現が出てきます。ですが，実験に協力・参加してくれる相手に失礼な表現であるということで，現在では participant（実験参加者）という表現を用いることになっています。

Random Assignment：ランダム・アサインメント（無作為割りつけ）

1.5 Why Not Use Introspection?

So far, you have learned that social psychologists use experiments as their primary research tool to examine theories involving causal relationships. Yet, unlike other animals (or even human babies), it is possible that human adults can verbally explain the real motivations behind their behaviors. If so, isn't **introspection** (i.e., asking participants to carefully observe and report their own mental states) a more straightforward research tool than experimentation? The answer is NO: although people readily provide reasonable causal explanations for their thoughts, feelings, and actions, their explanations are often quite inaccurate. This fact was first established by a landmark paper published by two social psychologists, Nisbett and Wilson (1977**a**).

Perhaps the most telling counterevidence against the validity of introspection was demonstrated in a study of the **halo effect** (see Nisbett & Wilson, 1977**b**, for details of this study). Researchers presented participants with either one of two videotaped interviews of a teacher who spoke English with a French accent.[1] In one video, the teacher was warm and friendly when answering questions, while in the other video, the teacher answered the same questions but gave cold and distrustful responses. Following exposure to either one of these videos, participants were asked to rate the teacher's likeability. As you may expect, participants liked the warm teacher much better than the cold teacher. In addition, participants were asked to rate the teacher's physical appearance, mannerisms, and accent, all of which were invariant (i.e., the exact same) in both videos. Somewhat surprisingly, participants rated these identical attributes more favorably in the warm condition than in the cold condition. In other words, global likeability influenced ratings of unrelated attributes—the halo effect!

The researchers, furthermore, asked some participants to introspect about whether likeability influenced their ratings of the teacher's attributes. The answer should be YES. However, as shown in Figure 1-3, the majority of participants considered that likeability had no effect on the three attribute ratings. Thus, participants were unaware of the halo effect. By contrast, another group of participants were asked whether the teacher's attributes (e.g., accent) influenced their ratings of teacher likeability. Notice that this is the causal opposite of the halo effect, and remember that the teacher's attributes did not change across conditions. Nonetheless, as shown in Figure 1-4, participants (especially in the cold condition) tended to consider that the teacher's attributes, as opposed to his warm or cold behavior, either increased or decreased their liking for him. Taken together, this experiment clearly demonstrates that people are often incapable of accurately reporting the true causes of their opinions. For this reason, social psychologists rely on experiments, not introspection.

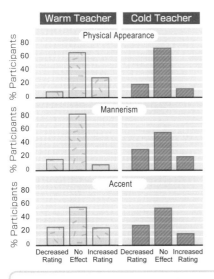 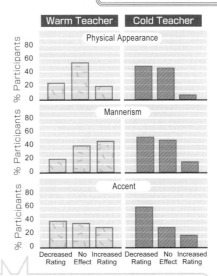

Figure 1-3は，先生の好ましさが先生の見た目，しぐさ，なまりの評価に影響しなかった（no effect）と多くの参加者が回答したことを示しています。その一方で，Figure 1-4は，先生の見た目，しぐさ，なまりが先生の好ましさに影響した（特に Cold Teacher 条件で好ましさを下げた）と回答したことを示しています。

Figure **1**-3. Participants' reports on whether global likeability increased or decreased their rating of each attribute (awareness of the halo effect). [Nisbett & Wilson, 1977b]

Figure **1**-4. Participants' reports on whether their rating of each attribute increased or decreased global likeability. [Nisbett & Wilson, 1977b]

Introspection：内観または内省　　実験の参加者に，自分の心的状態を注意深く観察して報告してもらうという研究方法です。ドイツのライプチッヒに世界最初の心理学実験室をつくった Wilhelm Wundt もこの方法を利用していました。

1997**a**, 1997**b**：この発表年の後の a と b は，論文固有のものではありません。同じ著者で同じ年に発表された論文を引用する場合に区別できないので，本文に出てきた順に 1997a, 1997b というふうにして 2 つの論文を区別できるようにしています。

Halo Effect：ハロー効果　　ある対象について目立ってよい特徴があると，その対象のほかの特徴もよいもののように思えることです（目立って悪い特徴のせいでほかの特徴も悪く思えることにも使われることがあります）。辞書的には halo の訳語は「後光」で，後光がさして見えるというニュアンスです。

1　Accent：なまり　　日本語では単語の強勢をアクセントといいますが，アメリカ英語では単語の強勢のことは stress といいます。

> **Advanced Topic**
>
> ## The Person-Situation Interaction

Although social psychology emphasizes the importance of situational influence, many social psychologists admit that more accurate explanations of human behavior incorporate the **person-situation interaction**. The person-situation interaction basically means that the same situation exerts different influences on different kinds of people.

Two social psychologists, Simpson and Willer (2008), surmised that people help others for at least two different dispositional reasons. Whereas some people are generally altruistic in nature, and are inclined to help others, some people are generally selfish, and are only inclined to help when it pays. To assay for these individual differences, the researchers first administered a **social value orientation** measure (Van Lange, 1999). This measure asks participants to make various hypothetical resource distributions between themselves and a partner. For example, if you prefer the option of giving both you and your partner 480 points over the option of giving 540 points to yourself but only 280 points to your partner, you would be classified as a "**prosocial**" person. If you prefer the second option to the first option, however, you would be classified as a "selfish" person.

Next, Simpson and Willer asked their participants to play a series of games in which real money was at stake. First, participants were instructed to divide $8 between themselves and their partner (X), in any amount they wished. Each participant was then paired with a new partner (Y) who would decide how much money (this time out of $12) he or she wished to give to the participant. These games were played under the following two conditions: In the *public condition*, Y was informed of how much money participants had given to X. In the *private condition*, by comparison, Y did not know how much money participants had given to X.

The results of Simpson and Willer's experiment are depicted in Figure 1–5. Prosocial people gave relatively high amounts to X regardless of the public/private condition (an effect of person). Furthermore, both prosocial and selfish people gave more money to X in the public condition than in the private condition (an effect of situation). This second effect makes sense: It is likely that participants assumed that Y would give little money to selfish people. In order to not look like a selfish person in the eyes of Y, participants thus gave more money to X in the public condition. In the private condition, such a concern for reputation-building did not arise.

Simpson and Willer further predicted a person-situation interaction effect: Selfish people were more influenced by the incentive for reputation-building than prosocial people. From the private condition to the public condition, prosocial participants' transfers increased only slightly (from $3.2 to $4), while selfish participants' transfers were more than doubled (from $1.8 to $3.7).

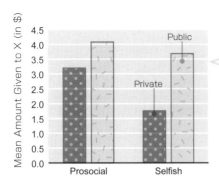

Figure 1-5. The amount of money given to X as a function of participant type and public/private condition. [Simpson & Willer, 2008]

Person-Situation Interaction：人と状況のインタラクション　　インタラクションは統計用語としては交互作用（Figure 1-5 の吹き出しを参照）と訳し，それ以外の場合には相互作用と訳します。例えば，2 人の人が会話をしたりする場合には相互作用です。

　人と状況のインタラクションの場合，統計用語ではありませんが，意味している内容は統計の交互作用効果（interaction effect）と同じです。人の特性（例えば性格）と状況要因の組み合わせによって結果が違ってくるということです。本書では，カタカナでインタラクションと表記しています。

Social Value Orientation：社会的価値志向性　　本文では簡単な説明にとどめていますが，本当は次のような 3 つの選択肢を提示し，どれが一番よいかを尋ねます。

　　　　A：自分は 480，相手は 80
　　　　B：自分は 540，相手は 280
　　　　C：自分も相手も 480

　A を選ぶ人は競争的，B を選ぶ人はエゴイスティック，C を選ぶ人は向社会的な社会価値志向性をもっているとされます。Simpson & Willer (2008) の研究では，参加者にこのような選択を 9 回してもらい，A または B を選ぶ傾向があった参加者をまとめて利己的 (selfish) な人として分類しました。

Prosocial：向社会的（または順社会的）　　Antisocial（反社会的）の反対の意味の言葉として社会心理学者が主に使っています。Prosocial behavior（向社会的行動）は広い意味でのよい行動を指します。例えば，相手と自分の両方の利益を考慮する平等なふるまいもよい行動のひとつです（CHAPTER 9 で詳しく扱います）。

References

Keizer, K., Lindenberg, S., & Steg, L. (2008). The spreading of disorder, *Science, 322,* 1681-1685. doi: 10.1126/science.1161405

Nisbett, R. E., & Wilson, T. D. (1977a). Telling more than we can know: Verbal reports on mental processes. *Psychological Review, 84,* 231-259. doi: 10.1037/0033-295X.84.3.231

Nisbett, R. E., & Wilson, T. D. (1977b). The halo effect: Evidence for unconscious alteration of judgments. *Journal of Personality and Social Psychology, 35,* 250-256. doi: 10.1037/0022-3514.35.4.250

Simpson, B., & Willer, R. (2008). Altruism and indirect reciprocity: The interaction of person and situation in prosocial behavior. *Social Psychology Quarterly, 71,* 37-52. doi: 10.1177/019027250807100106

Van Lange, P. A. M. (1999). The pursuit of joint outcomes and equality of outcomes: An integrative model of social value orientation. *Journal of Personality and Social Psychology, 77,* 337-349. doi: 10.1037/0022-3514.77.2.337

📖 引用文献の表記法　　本書では，本文中で紹介した論文の書誌情報をアメリカ心理学会（American Psychological Association: APA）のマニュアルにしたがって記載します。

　論文の場合は，最初に著者名（family name を書き，first name や middle name はイニシャルにします）を列挙し，出版年を括弧にいれて記載します。次にくるのが論文タイトルです。タイトルの後に，斜体で論文が掲載されている雑誌名を書きます。雑誌名の後には，その論文が掲載されている巻（volume）を斜体で書きます。その後に，掲載されている最初のページと最後のページをハイフンでつなぐかたちで記載します。

　最後についている doi というのは，digital object identifier の略で，その論文のインターネット上の住所のようなものです。http://dx.doi.org/ の後にこの doi 番号をつけてインターネットのブラウザのアドレス欄にいれると，その論文のサイトにとびます。ただし，論文を読めるかどうかは，その雑誌がどの範囲の人に論文を公開しているかによるので注意してください。現在はオープンアクセスといって，誰でも読める雑誌が増えてきていますが，そうではない雑誌のほうがまだまだ多い状況です。その場合は，大学などが出版社と契約してお金を払っていないと読むことができません。ただし，論文の要旨（abstract）だけは契約によらず読むことができます。

　外国人の著者の場合，どちらが family name（姓）でどちらが first name（名）かわかりにくいかもしれません。雑誌論文では，通常，タイトルのすぐ下あたりに著者名が書かれています。雑誌にもよりますが，原則として first name が先，family name が後と覚えておくとよいでしょう。この原則が守られないとき（family name 先，first name 後）のときには，family name の後にコンマが入っているのが一般的です。例えば，日本語の名前（Yohsuke Ohtsubo）については次のようになります。

　　　一般的な順序での表記：Yohsuke Ohtsubo
　　　順序を入れ替えて表記：Ohtsubo, Yohsuke

論文を引用するときには著者の family name のほうを使います。

CHAPTER 2

Self
自己

2.1
What is the Self?

2.2
Self-Schema: The Cognitive Structure of Self

2.3
Positive Illusions and Mental Health

2.4
Social Comparison and Self-Evaluation

2.5
Self-Esteem Tracks Others' Valuation of the Self

Advanced Topic
Self-Regulation and Delay of Gratification

2.1 What is the Self?

What is the self? This sounds like a philosophical question. In fact, a philosopher and forerunner of modern psychology, William James (1890) famously distinguished two aspects of the self: "*I*" (the knower) and "*me*" (the known). The "*I*" self is the center of subjective consciousness that unites a continuous stream of experiences. The "*me*" self is more objective. For example, you can touch your leg, which is objectively distinguishable from someone else's leg.

Taking a somewhat different perspective, the sociologist, Cooley (1902), argued that one of the most important sources of our self-concept is other people. In the same way as our appearance is revealed by reference to a looking glass, Cooley purported that we understand ourselves by how other people view us. This is called the **looking-glass self**. Despite these theoretical differences, however, both James and Cooley agree that the self is understood through our experiences (be they personal or interpersonal).

Human adults no doubt have self-concepts, but can young children and other animals also recognize the self? To answer this question empirically, Gallup (1970) developed a research method called the **mirror test**. This involves putting a red mark on an animal's face (while the animal **isn't** paying attention), placing the animal in front of a mirror, and observing how the animal reacts to its reflection. In the case of a chimpanzee, although it might not immediately recognize the reflection as itself, the chimp will eventually do the following—it will touch the red mark *not* on the mirror image, but on its own face! In other words, it will recognize that the image in the mirror is a reflection of itself. A developmental psychologist, Amsterdam (1972), applied a similar procedure to human children ages 6 to 24 months. The results showed that the majority of children between ages 20 and 24 months (but not younger) recognize the mirror image as themselves.

Of course, the second year of life is only the starting point in the journey to self-understanding. Once people start talking and writing, we can ask them to verbally describe who they are. A research method called the **Twenty Statements Test**, for example, asks respondents to write up to twenty sentences starting with the words "I am ..." (Kuhn & McPartland, 1954). This method reveals that common self-concepts include attributes such as name, age, gender, possessions, personality, and behavior.

In this chapter, we will learn how social psychologists have investigated self-concepts (also known as self-schema). We will discuss how certain illusions regarding the self may affect mental health, and we will explore how comparing oneself with others can both help and hinder a sense of well-being. Finally, we will consider the social dynamics of self-esteem and the importance of self-regulation.

"I" と "Me"：主我と客我　　James（1890）は自己（self）を主我（*I*）と客我（*Me*）に分けて考えることを提唱しました。本文では省略していますが，客我は物質的自己（material self）・社会的自己（social self）・精神的自己（spiritual self）の3つからなるとJamesは考えました。物質的自己とは自分の身体や持ち物のことです。社会的自己とは他者から認識されている自己です。Jamesは，厳密に考えれば他者の数だけ社会的自己があると述べています。精神的自己とは性格など内面的な部分で，他の2種類の自己よりも変化しにくいものだと考えられています。

Looking-Glass Self：鏡映的自己

Mirror Test：ミラーテスト　　Gallup（1970）によって考案されたこのテストは，赤いマークを顔につけるということからマークテストと呼ばれたり，赤という色にちなんでルージュテスト（rouge test）と呼ばれることもあります。

📖　**～ not の短縮形**　　本書ではあまりにも堅苦しい表現にしないために～ not の短縮形を使用している箇所があります。しかし，学術論文では **isn't**，don't，won't 等の短縮形は使いません。また，助動詞 can の否定では can と not の間にスペースを入れずに cannot と書くのが一般的です。

Twenty Statements Test：20答法

2.2 Self-Schema: The Cognitive Structure of Self

Knowing about the self (or *me* in James's terminology) usually involves knowing one's name, birthday, birthplace, personality, hobbies, aptitudes, and so on. These are not scattered pieces of knowledge, but comprise a well-organized structure called a **self-schema** (Markus, 1977). The term, **schema**, is borrowed from cognitive psychology, a subfield of psychology devoted to the study of information processing (e.g., memory, learning). In cognitive psychology, it is assumed that any piece of knowledge is stored in our memory in relation to other pieces of knowledge. Such interrelated knowledge comprises a cognitive structure, which is formally called a schema.

It is well known that structured knowledge facilitates faster information processing. Applying this general principle of cognitive psychology to self-schema, a social psychologist, Markus (1977), pioneered experimental research on the self. Markus made use of the presence of individual differences in self-schemas: some people see the independent-dependent dimension of personality as self-relevant, but others consider this dimension irrelevant to themselves. Based on personality assessment of participants' level of independence (or dependence), Markus categorized her participants into three groups: *Independents*, *Dependents*, and *Aschematics* who saw themselves as neither independent nor dependent.

Three to four weeks after the personality assessment, participants engaged in several experimental tasks. In one task, participants were presented a set of various adjectives, some were related to independence and others were related to dependence. Participants were then asked to judge whether the adjectives described themselves, or not, as quickly as possible. Markus measured participants' **response/reaction time** (**RT**), which is also known as **latency**, to both independent adjectives (e.g., individualistic, self-confident) and dependent adjectives (e.g., conforming, submissive).

As Markus expected, self-relevance facilitated (i.e., increased the speed of) participants' responses. Dependents responded to dependent adjectives faster than to independent adjectives (compare the two left-hand bars in Figure 2-1). By contrast, independents responded to independent adjectives faster than to dependent adjectives (compare the two right-hand bars). In addition, Aschematics did not differ in their response time to either set of adjectives (compare the two middle bars). These results clearly demonstrate that individual differences in self-schema have an important effect on information processing.

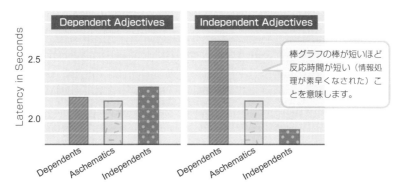

Figure 2-1. Mean latency for dependent and independent adjectives for the three types of participants. [Markus, 1977]

Schema：スキーマ　認知心理学（cognitive psychology）の用語で，構造化された知識のことを意味しています。ものごとの手続き（例えば，「レストランに入った後に，席に案内され，メニューを見て，注文し，食事が運ばれてきたら，それを食べて，お会計をして店を出る」という一連の流れ）についてのスキーマのことは，特に**スクリプト**（**script**）と呼ばれています。

同様に自己についての構造化された知識のことを**自己スキーマ**（**self-schema**）といいます。Markus は，1977 年の論文で，自己スキーマを次のように定義しています（Markus, 1977, p. 64）。

> Self-schemata are cognitive generalizations about the self, derived from past experience, that organize and guide the processing of self-related information contained in the individual's social experiences.

この定義の主語になっている self-schemata は self-schema の複数形です。この定義で重要なポイントは，自己スキーマが経験によって形成されるという点，自己スキーマをもっていることで自己に関連する情報が効率的に処理されるようになるということです。

Response/Reaction Time（RT）：反応時間

Latency：反応潜時（反応時間と同義）

2.3 Positive Illusions and Mental Health

How well do you really know yourself? Traditionally, psychologists have considered accurate self-perception to be a hallmark of mental health. Imagine that someone seriously declares, "I am God and I will live forever." Such a grandiose statement would appear to be a symptom of some mental illness, not exactly something a healthy person would say. Therefore, it seems valid to assume that *accurate* self-perception ought to be associated with mental health.

In 1988, two social psychologists, Taylor and Brown, challenged this "truism" of the psychological community. One of the authors, Taylor, had been studying the coping behaviors of cancer patients, and had noticed that better adjusted patients held some rather biased, yet positive, beliefs (e.g., "[I can] personally prevent the cancer from coming back," Taylor & Brown, 1988, p. 201). Integrating such observations with other well-established findings in the field of social cognition (CHAPTER 3), Taylor and Brown proposed that mental health is characterized not by accurate self-perceptions, but rather by so-called **positive illusions**.

Positive illusions consist of three positively biased self-related perceptions: "*unrealistically* positive self-evaluations, *exaggerated* perceptions of control or mastery, and *unrealistic* optimism" (Taylor & Brown, 1988, p. 193, **emphases added**). First, an abundance of evidence shows that ordinary (i.e., mentally healthy) people tend to view themselves more favorably (e.g., as kinder, warmer) than other people. For example, most people tend to report that positive personality traits are more descriptive of themselves than of the average person (despite the logical impossibility of this state of affairs).

Second, people tend to feel like they have some control over events that are largely determined by chance (e.g., gambling). This phenomenon is called the **illusion of control**. Third, people tend to think that they are more likely than their peers to experience positive events, such as getting a good salary or having a gifted child.

Taylor and Brown argued that exhibiting these three types of positive illusions is actually associated with sound mental health. For example, compared to people who lack these illusions, people with positive illusions tend to be happier as well as better at coping with medical difficulties.

In a more recent paper, Taylor and Brown (1994) make some important caveats. They are careful to state that illusions do not cure diseases (although they can help people cope). They also introduce an important boundary condition: positive illusions are only useful at a mild level—extremely distorted self-perceptions may be symptomatic of psychopathology. Thus, it may be better phrased that holding *mild* positive illusions is a common psychological phenomenon that is associated with good mental health.

Positive Illusions：ポジティヴ・イリュージョン　　Taylor & Brown（1988）は，現実よりも肯定的な自己評価，現実よりも過剰な自己の統制感，将来についての楽観的なとらえかたの3つをポジティヴ・イリュージョンとして精神的に健康な人に一般に見られる認知の偏りであると考えました。

認知の偏りはバイアス（bias）やエラー（error）ともいいます。ですが，Taylor & Brown は，ポジティヴ・イリュージョンを多くの人が共通に現実を見誤る錯視（visual illusion）に近いものと考え，illusion という用語をあてました。

日本語ではポジティヴ・イリュージョンですが，英語では3つをセットにしているので複数形の positive illusions になっていることに気をつけてください。

📖 引用の決まり　　他の研究者の考えや実験結果を参考にして文章を書くときには，参考にした論文を明記しなければなりません。例えば，本文の中で「Taylor and Brown（1994）」や「(Taylor & Brown, 1988)」と書いているのがそれです。各章の最後につけている引用文献一覧（references）を見ると，それぞれの論文がどの雑誌の何巻に掲載されているかがわかります。

　　単に考えや実験結果を参考にしただけでなく，元の論文の中の文章をそのまま引用するときにはシングル・クォーテーション・マーク（' '），またはダブル・クォーテーション・マーク（" "）でくくります（前者はイギリス英語，後者はアメリカ英語のルールです）。

　　文章を引用したときには，元の論文のページ数も「p. 193」のように示します。引用箇所が複数のページにまたがるときには「pp. 193-194」のように表記します（ただし，複数ページにまたがるような長い引用の場合は，クォーテーション・マークでくくるのでではなく，インデントを使って（字下げして）独立した段落として記載するのが一般的です）。Section 2.2 では，Markus（1977）による self-schema の定義をこの形式で引用しています。

　　また，この Section 2.3 では，引用した文章にもともとの論文にはない斜体（イタリック）の強調を加えています。そのことを示すために，「**emphases added**（強調は〔原文にないものが〕加えられた）」とただし書きをつけています。

Illusion of Control：コントロール幻想

2.4 Social Comparison and Self-Evaluation

It is not enough to succeed. Others must fail. — Gore Vidal

For better or worse, people have a natural tendency to compare themselves to other people in their social environment (Festinger, 1954). We usually compare ourselves to people around us such as family members, friends, classmates, and coworkers, though we may also find ourselves making comparisons to figures from literature or mass media such as the protagonists of stories or the actors and actresses who portray them on screen. Importantly, we often choose the targets of our **social comparison** in service of ourselves.

One of the major functions of social comparison is **self-evaluation**. By comparing the self with the right targets, we attain a better understanding of ourselves. However, accurate self-assessment is not the only motivation for social comparison.

There are two basic types of social comparison, downward comparisons and upward comparisons (Wills, 1981). A **downward social comparison** happens when we compare ourselves to people we consider worse off than ourselves. For example, imagine one of your peers who is not doing very well, who often fails at achieving some important goal. Although thinking about this person's failure may make you feel sorry for this person, insofar as you perform a downward social comparison, you are likely to feel better about yourself. There is even a special word for the feeling that occurs when we reflect on the failure of others and take pleasure in their misfortune, **schadenfreude**.

An **upward social comparison** occurs when we compare ourselves to people we consider better off than ourselves, and usually leads us to feel relatively bad. For example, comparing yourself with someone much wealthier than yourself would likely make you feel miserable. Nevertheless, there is a potential upside to upward comparisons: they can act as powerful motivators for change. Indeed, many people purposely surround themselves with images of their idols or heroes in order to motivate themselves to improve their lives.

Wood, Taylor, and Lichtman (1985) interviewed breast cancer patients about their social comparison targets (see also Section 2.3 on positive illusions). The results revealed that most patients engage in downward social comparison—they tend to compare themselves to more misfortunate individuals. For example, many patients favorably compared themselves with others who had to undergo "awful" surgeries such as a mastectomy (i.e., a complete removal of one or both breasts), and older patients often favorably compared themselves with younger, relatively less fortunate, patients. These results suggest that downward comparison may serve as a coping strategy for people who are under adverse conditions.

Social Comparison：社会的比較　　Festinger（1954）は，人々には自己評価のために自分を他者と比べる傾向があると考え，社会的比較の理論を提唱しました。社会的比較は，その対象の立場や状況が自分より悪い，能力が自分より低い場合に**下方比較（downward comparison）**といい，相手の立場や状況が自分よりよい，能力が高い場合に**上方比較（upward comparison）**といいます。

　英語では本文の中で書いているように downward social comparison, upward social comparison ということもあれば，単に downward comparison, upward comparison ということもあります。ですが，日本語では下方比較，上方比較というのが一般的です。

Self-Evaluation：自己評価　　自分とはどのような人物であるかについて知ることを自己評価といいます。自己評価を行うことで，自己について正しく知り，自己をよりよくコントロールできるようになると考えられています。ただし，私たちはいつでも自己について正しく知りたいと思うわけではないようです。多くの社会心理学者は，自己評価過程には，少なくとも以下の3つの異なる動機づけが関係していると考えています（Sedikides & Strube, 1995）。

　　自己高揚動機（self-enhancement motive）：自分は他者より優れている，よりよいと感じたいという願望のことです。主に下方比較によって達成されると考えられます。

　　自己確証動機（self-verification motive）：自己概念の正しさを確認したいという願望です。自分の言うことを肯定してくれそうな相手とつき合うことなどで達成されます。

　　自己査定動機（self-assessment motive）：よいことであれ，悪いことであれ，自分について正しく知りたいという願望です。精度の高いテストを受けることなどで達成されます。

Schadenfreude：シャーデンフロイデ（ドイツ語の単語）

📖 **引用以外でのクォーテーション・マーク（" "）の使い方**　　他者の言葉を引用する以外にもクォーテーション・マークを使うことがあります。例えば，その部分を特に強調したいとき，その部分に特別なニュアンスがあること（反語表現や皮肉）を示すときに使います。

　今回は，手術に対して awful という形容詞を使いましたが，手術の中に患者さんに苦痛を与えるために行われる本当に awful なものがあると考えているわけではありません。しかし，ある種の手術（乳がんで乳房全体を切除するような手術）を患者さんは awful と感じるでしょう。手術が awful だというのは，あくまでも患者さんの主観的な評価だ，というニュアンスを示すためにクォーテーション・マークを使っています。

2.5 Self-Esteem Tracks Others' Valuation of the Self

Social psychologists use the term **self-esteem** to describe a person's valuation of him/herself. It is usually an affectively-laden term—people feel good about themselves when they favorably appraise themselves. Accordingly, high self-esteem is linked to high subjective well-being, while low self-esteem is related to mental illness.

Recall that people have a motivation to protect and promote their self-esteem (see Section 2.4 regarding the "self-enhancement motive"). Moreover, we appear to have some biases for seeing ourselves in a positive light compared to others (see Section 2.3 regarding "positive illusions"). Given the presence of these self-oriented predispositions, one might wonder why on earth self-esteem should ever go down. Isn't it a good idea to have some psychological mechanism that keeps self-esteem always high?

This is in fact a misguided idea. Self-esteem is important not for its own sake, but for its relation to some real, social, consequences. Leary and Baumeister (2000) proposed the **sociometer theory**, whereby self-esteem is conceived as "a subjective monitor of one's relational evaluation—the degree to which other people regard their relationships with the individual to be valuable, important, or close" (Leary & Baumeister, 2000, p. 9). According to the sociometer theory, self-esteem fluctuates as a reflection of other people's evaluations, but not in response to one's own non-social evaluation.

If the sociometer theory is valid, self-esteem should go down when an individual experiences social exclusion. Leary, Tambor, Terdal, and Downs (1995), in fact, tested this prediction with an experiment employing **a 2** (exclusion: included vs. excluded) **× 2** (assignment: random vs. group choice) **factorial design**. To start, participants were told that they would engage in either a group decision-making task or an individual decision-making task. After this instruction, a quarter of participants were told that they were assigned to engage in the group task because other members wanted to work with them. Another quarter were told that they were assigned to engage in the individual task because other people did not want to work with them. The remaining half were told that they had been randomly assigned to the group or individual task.

As shown in Figure 2-2, the results of Leary et al.'s experiment confirm the main prediction from the sociometer theory that self-esteem is calibrated in response to information about one's social standing. Participants felt bad about themselves (i.e., experienced decreases in self-esteem) only in the excluded-group choice condition, which implies that they were not valued by other group members. Working alone due to random assignment (i.e., the excluded-random condition) did not hurt self-esteem. Therefore, it is clear that while simply being alone matters little for self-esteem, being alone due to others' social disregard is potentially devastating.

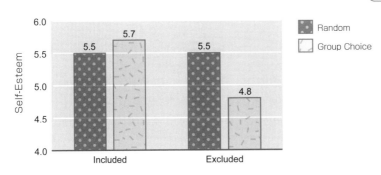

Figure 2-2. Mean self-esteem as a function of exclusion and the mode of assignment. [Leary et al., 1995 より筆者作成]

Self-Esteem：自尊感情　本文中では自尊感情が他者の評価によって変動することを示した研究を紹介しています。厳密にいうと，このように変動しやすい自尊感情は状態自尊感情（state self-esteem）と呼ばれます。

それに対して，世の中にはそもそも自尊感情の高い人，低い人がいて，このような個人差は多少のことでは変化しません。自尊感情の中でも長期的に安定している部分を特性自尊感情（trait self-esteem）といいます。

Leary et al. (1995) の論文では，普段からみんなに受け入れられていると感じているかどうかの違いが特性自尊心の高低と関係していることを示した研究も報告されています。

Sociometer Theory：ソシオメーター理論

📖 **実験デザインの表記法**　論文で報告されている実験の概要は，それがどのような要因配置（factorial design）の実験であるかを知ることでわかりやすくなります。必ず書かれているわけではありませんが，**a 2** (Condition A) **× 2** (Condition B) **factorial design** のように書かれていれば，この実験には2つの条件が含まれていて，それぞれに2水準あることがわかります。一方が2水準，他方が3水準なら2×3になりますし，2水準の条件が3つ含まれる場合は2×2×2になります。括弧の中には，それぞれの条件がどのようなものかが簡単に書かれています。これは，卒業論文など自分で論文を書くときにも使える表現です。

Advanced Topic: Self-Regulation and Delay of Gratification

The classic research question for **self-regulation** involves explaining why people are somewhat poor at **delaying gratification**; in particular, why people are often willing to exchange a small reward now for a larger, better, reward that comes later. This sort of self-regulation problem manifests in daily life all the time. For example, imagine you are on a diet trying to lose 5 kilograms, and a friend offers you some fried chicken. Do you eat the fried chicken now, and experience the pleasure of the food, or do you turn down the temptation now, in order to experience the eventual satisfaction of losing weight in the future (i.e., **delayed gratification**)? Or, imagine you are at home working on an important **term paper**. Then, out of nowhere your friend invites you to play a brand new videogame. Do you play the videogame with your friend, or do you decline the offer and continue to work on your paper? While it is obvious in these examples that waiting for a *"larger, later"* reward is the rational choice, we sometimes surrender ourselves to the *"smaller, sooner"* reward. Intuitively, there seem to be large individual differences in the ability to delay gratification.

Mischel and colleagues designed a simple yet clever experiment on the delay of gratification, commonly called the **marshmallow test** (see Mischel, Shoda, & Rodriguez, 1989, for a review). Before leaving a preschool child alone in a room, a researcher presents the child with two sorts of snacks (marshmallows and pretzels, for example), and asks which of the two snacks the child likes better. The child is told if he/she wishes to eat a snack, he/she can ring a bell, and the experimenter will come back immediately at which point the child will be allowed to eat the less preferred snack. If the child can wait until the experimenter comes back (unbeknownst to the child, this time is set to 15 minutes), however, the child will be allowed to eat the preferred snack.

Mischel and colleagues timed how long each child was able to wait before ringing the bell, and revealed that many children had a very difficult time in this experimental setting. Indeed, there were large individual differences in how long children were able to wait. Nevertheless, the original studies have also revealed that the presence of distractors (e.g., attractive toys) can help children wait longer.

Another interesting set of findings emerged from a series of follow-up studies. Delay of gratification measured at 4 years of age predicted how parents described their children 10 years later—children who had been able to wait longer in the original experiment were seen as more socially competent, verbally fluent in expressing their ideas, and resilient to stress. Delayed gratification even predicted the children's **Scholastic Aptitude Test (SAT)** scores. Of course, these results are just correlations, but the connection between self-regulation and success in life is difficult to deny.

Self-Regulation：自己制御

Delay of Gratification：満足の遅延　　将来得られる大きな報酬（larger, later）のために，すぐに得られる小さな報酬（smaller, sooner）をがまんすることです。報酬によって満足を得るタイミングを先送りにするという意味で，満足の遅延といいます。インターネットで **delayed gratification** や **delaying gratification** というキーワードを使って検索をしても，Mischelらの研究が出てきます。

📖 **Term paper**　　日本の大学でレポート課題と呼んでいるものは，アメリカでは term paper（または省略して paper）といいます。また，日本で論述式の試験というのは essay 形式と呼ばれます（日本語の「エッセイ」とは少しニュアンスが違います）。実験の課題としてこれらのレポートを課したり，論述作業をしてもらうという研究もあり，その場合はこれらの表現が心理学の論文に出てきます。覚えておくと論文が読みやすくなります（Section 3.2 の 📖 も参照）。

Marshmallow Test：マシュマロ・テスト　　マシュマロ・テストについての一般読者向けの記事を *New Yorker* 誌の下記のサイトで読むことができます。"The Struggles of a Psychologist Studying Self-Control" というタイトルで検索してみてください。
　　http://www.newyorker.com/science/maria-konnikova/struggles-psychologist-studying-self-control

📖 **See ... for a review**　　特定のテーマについてこれまで行われてきた研究結果をまとめて整理した論文を review 論文（レヴュー論文または展望論文）といいます。ある研究テーマについての review 論文を参考にして下さいという意味で "see 論文の著者名, 発表年, for a review" という表現が使われます。

📖 **Scholastic Aptitude Test（SAT）**　　アメリカで実施されている大学進学用の共通試験です（大学進学適正試験と訳されています）。Mischelらの論文が発表された後，名称が Scholastic Assessment Test に変更されています。ただし，変更後も略称は SAT です。
　　心理学の論文でも，実験参加者の学力の指標として SAT score という言葉が特に注釈もつけずに出てくることがあります。

References

Amsterdam, B. (1972). Mirror self-image reactions before age two. *Developmental Psychobiology, 5*, 297-305. doi: 10.1002/dev.420050403

Cooley, C. H. (1902). *Human nature and the social order.* New York: Charles Scribner's Son.

Festinger, L. (1954). A theory of social comparison processes. *Human Relations, 7*, 117-140. doi: 10.1177/001872675400700202

Gallup, G. G., Jr. (1970). Chimpanzees: Self recognition. *Science, 167*, 86-87. doi: 10.1126/science.167.3914.86

James, W. (1890). *The principles of psychology.* New York: Holt.

Kuhn, M. H., & McPartland, T. S. (1954). An empirical investigation of self-attitudes. *American Sociological Review, 19*, 68-76. Retrieved from http://www.jstor.org/stable/2088175

Leary, M. R., & Baumesiter, R. F. (2000). The nature and function of self-esteem: Sociometer theory. In M. P. Zanna (Ed.), *Advances in experimental social psychology*, Vol. 32 (pp. 1-62). San Diego, CA: Academic Press. doi: 10.1016/S0065-2601(00)80003-9

Leary, M. R., Tambor, E. S., Terdal, S. K., & Downs, D. L. (1995). Self-esteem as an interpersonal monitor: The sociometer hypothesis. *Journal of Personality and Social Psychology, 68*, 518-530. doi: 10.1037/0022-3514.68.3.518

Markus, H. (1977). Self-schemata and processing information about the self. *Journal of Personality and Social Psychology, 35*, 63-78. doi: 10.1037/0022-3514.35.2.63

Mischel, W., Shoda, Y., & Rodriguez, M. L. (1989). Delay of gratification in children. *Science, 244*, 933-938. doi: 10.1126/science.2658056

Sedikides, C., & Strube, M. J. (1995). The multiply motivated self. *Personality and Social Psychology Bulletin, 21*, 1330-1335. doi: 10.1177/01461672952112010

Taylor, S. E., & Brown, J. D. (1988). Illusion and well-being: A social psychological perspective on mental health. *Psychological Bulletin, 103*, 193-210. doi: 10.1037/0033-2909.103.2.193

Taylor, S. E., & Brown, J. D. (1994). Positive illusions and well-being revisited: Separating fact from fiction. *Psychological Bulletin, 116*, 21-27. doi: 10.1037/0033-2909.116.1.21

Wills, T. A. (1981). Downward comparison principles in social psychology. *Psychological Bulletin, 90*, 245-271. doi: 10.1037/0033-2909.90.2.245

Wood, J. V., Taylor, S. E., & Lichtman, R. R. (1985). Social comparison in adjustment to breast cancer. *Journal of Personality and Social Psychology, 49*, 1169-1183. doi: 10.1037/0022-3514.49.5.1169

CHAPTER 3

Social Cognition
社会的認知

3.1
How Well Do Our Thoughts Reflect Reality?

3.2
Errors in Causal Attributions

3.3
Prior Knowledge Influences Perception

3.4
Illusory Correlation

3.5
Heuristics and Cognitive Biases

Advanced Topic
The Accuracy of Social Cognition

3.1 How Well Do Our Thoughts Reflect Reality?

In this chapter we will present scientific findings related to cognitive (i.e., thought-related) processes that occur in individual minds yet within the context of society—**social cognition**. It will become clear that much of our social cognition is apparently erroneous. In other words, a lot of information processing seems to be subject to, at times serious, mistakes. As a result, thoughts often fail to reflect reality.

How can this be so? Take, as an example, a **purported** memory experiment, where participants were presented with a technical article describing the connection between caffeine consumption and fibrocystic disease,[1] which in its advanced stage is associated with breast cancer (Kunda, 1987). The article explained the underlying mechanism: caffeine consumption causes concentration of a particular substance, called cAMP, in the breast. After reading this article, participants were asked about several aspects of the article, including two critical questions. First, participants were asked how much they were convinced about the connection between caffeine consumption and the disease. Second, they were asked about their own level of caffeine consumption.

The results clearly demonstrate the **self-serving bias** that occurs when interpreting scientific evidence. As shown in Figure 3-1, members of the **alleged** high-risk group (i.e., females who consume high amounts of caffeine) were **significantly** less convinced by the evidence than other participants (i.e., males; females who consume low amounts of caffeine). The high risk group members protected the integrity of their self-identities by underestimating the validity of the scientific evidence.

As we have already discussed (see CHAPTER 2), cognition is often distorted in service of the self. However, self-preservation is not the only source of biases. As information from the outside world (the social world in particular) is almost overwhelmingly complex, it is impossible to process everything in a piecemeal fashion. Thus our minds rely on simpler, and thereby more manageable, cognitive processes. For example, we may make *a priori* assumptions to expedite laborious information processing. Or we may employ some reasoning routines to save a substantial amount of time in reaching our conclusions about other people.

Such streamlined cognitive processes, though useful for navigating the complex social world, often mislead us—we may fall prey to **systematic** cognitive biases. Fortunately, for those of us who study social psychology, the systematic nature of our cognitive biases means that the mistakes we make are more or less predictable. Therefore, after reading this chapter, we hope you will gain not only an awareness of the many pitfalls inherent to our social cognition, but also an understanding of how to avoid them.

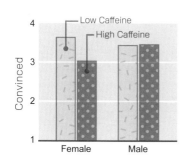

Figure 3-1. Average responses (female vs. male / low vs. high caffeine consumption) to a question about the extent to which participants were convinced by the information in the article. [Kunda, 1987]

Social Cognition：社会的認知　社会心理学の中でも特に認知心理学に影響を受けた分野で，社会的場面での人々の認知プロセスを研究しています。具体的には，対人的な知覚，記憶，推論などが研究対象となります。

📖　**実験の本当の目的を隠しているときの表現**　社会心理学では，本当の目的を参加者に伝えてしまうと実験結果に影響すると考えられるときに，真の目的を隠すことがあります。その場合，「参加者にはただの性格検査と伝えてある課題」というような表現が必要になります。このときによく使われるのが **purported** や **alleged** といった表現です。この副詞形の purportedly，allegedly もよく論文で使われています。

Self-Serving Bias：自己奉仕バイアス　ここでは自己奉仕バイアスは広い意味で使っています。狭い意味では，成功と失敗を自分に都合よく解釈することを指します。

📖　**Significant：有意な**　Significant という単語を辞書で引くと「重要な」と出てきます。ですが，心理学の論文に出てくる場合には大抵は統計用語として用いられていて，「有意な」と訳します。得られた結果が偶然で生じるとは考えにくいといった意味です。

📖　**Systematic：系統的な**　ランダムではなく規則性があるといったニュアンスです。バイアスとは回答パターンが規則性をもって偏ることで，規則性がなくばらつくエラーとは区別されます。

1　Fibrocystic Disease：乳腺症　　Kunda（1987）は，実際の医学雑誌を参考に記事を作成しました。ただし，カフェインと乳腺症の関係については，その後，否定的な論文が発表されたということです。女性の方はご安心ください。
　　余談ですが，認知的不協和理論（Section 6.2）で有名な Festinger は，ヘビースモーカーが喫煙とがんの関係を示す科学的データを不十分だと考えていることを見出し（1950 年代の話です），それを認知的不協和理論に基づき解釈しています（Festinger, 1957；書誌情報は CHAPTER 6 の References を参照）。

3.2 Errors in Causal Attributions

Think about the last time you did poorly on something, for example, when you got a poor grade on a test. What caused your poor performance? When answering this question, you may blame your own inability, but you are very likely to recall the various **external factors** (i.e., causes beyond your control such as obstacles, coercion, luck, etc.) that prevented you from succeeding (Heider, 1958). For example, you may blame a loud neighbor who interrupted your sleep, a roommate who convinced you to party instead of study, or a teacher who made the test too hard. In psychological terms, we call these external causal explanations of behavior **external attributions**.

Now, imagine that rather than yourself, another person in your class did poorly on the same test. Rather than go easy on this person by listing all the possible external factors that may have prevented him or her from succeeding, we tend to do the opposite. We tend to attribute the behavior of other people to **internal factors** (i.e., causes within a person's control) such as ability, attitude, effort, personality, and so on. Thus, we may claim that the student was lazy, immature, or simply unintelligent, in which case we would be making **internal attributions**.

This tendency to underestimate the importance of external factors when inferring the causes of others' behavior is known as the **fundamental attribution error** (or **correspondence bias**), which was first demonstrated in a classic study by Jones and Harris (1967). Participants were instructed to read an essay that either favorably or unfavorably described Fidel Castro[1] (the then-dictator of Cuba). Half of the participants were told that the writer had been assigned to take a particular position (either pro-Castro or anti-Castro) in writing the essay (the no choice condition), while the remaining participants were told that the writer had been allowed to take whatever position he/she preferred (the choice condition). You are correct if you think the essay in the no choice condition tells us nothing about the writer's internal attributes (e.g., his/her true attitude). Thus, it seems ridiculous to include the no choice condition in an attribution experiment. But let's see what happened.

The left-side of Figure 3-2 shows the result of the choice condition; it makes sense—participants who read the pro-Castro essay inferred that the writer had a pro-Castro attitude, while those who read the anti-Castro essay inferred the opposite. The right-side of the figure shows a somewhat surprising result. Although they were explicitly told that the position expressed in the essay was assigned by the experimenter, participants still believed that the writer's true attitude was similar to the position expressed in the essay. This result clearly shows that people tend to make internal attributions (i.e., tend to think that a person has an attitude congruent with his or her action), even when making an external attribution is the logical and right thing to do.

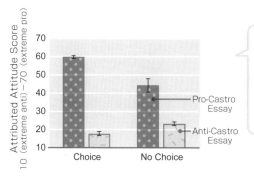

Figure 3-2. Participants' estimate of the essay writer's true attitude toward Castro. ［Jones & Harris, 1967 より筆者作成］

Attribution Theory：帰属理論　　ある人（自分も含む）がなぜある行動をしたのかを推論することを帰属といいます。例えば，「A さんが万引きをしたことを，A さんの家庭環境の悪さに帰属する」というふうにいいます。

　Heider（1958）は帰属理論を提唱し，社会的認知という言葉が使われる前から人々の認知（推論）について研究していました。Heider は，私たちが行う帰属は，行為者の**外的要因**（external factor）に帰属する**外的帰属**（external attribution）と**内的要因**（internal factor）に帰属する**内的帰属**（internal attribution）に大別できることを指摘しました。

　Attribute という単語は，動詞として「帰属する」という意味以外にも，名詞として「属性」（本文中の internal attributes）という意味でも使うので注意してください。

Fundamental Attribution Error：基本的帰属のエラー　　他者の行動を見たときに，外的要因を十分に考慮せずに，原因を内的に帰属しやすい傾向のことです。これを **correspondence bias**（対応バイアス）ということもあります。前 section でエラーは系統的なものではないと述べました。したがって，基本的帰属の"エラー"は厳密には系統的なバイアスです。

📖 **Essay**　　日本語ではエッセイといえば随想のことを意味しますが，英語では小論文や論述形式の試験の解答のような作文も指します。

1　Fidel Castro：フィデル・カストロ　　カストロは，キューバに社会主義政権をつくった革命家です。アメリカとの関係を絶ちソ連（当時）に接近したため，当時のアメリカではおおむね嫌われていました。

3.3 Prior Knowledge Influences Perception

What kind of image do you have of *Judo*[1] wrestlers? What kind of image do you have of nursery school teachers? How about lawyers? **It's** not hard to give an answer to these questions. **That's** because you have category-based knowledge about different groups of people. You believe that people in a certain category (e.g., *Judo* wrestlers) share some common characteristics that distinguish them from people in other categories. Such category-based understandings are called **stereotypes**. Of course, occupations are not the only social categories. Gender and race are other prominent social categories. We can imagine typical men or women. We even have stereotypes of people in subcategories of these social categories (e.g., "men from the Kyushu region or *Kyushu danji* are masculine").

Stereotypes tend to be considered a bad thing, as many times they are outright wrong. Even widely held stereotypes such as "men are taller than women," are potentially inaccurate. If you are talking about the average height of men and women, you are right, but, if you are talking about a particular man or woman, the stereotype may not hold. After all, there are many women who are taller than the average man, and there are many men who are shorter than the average woman.

If stereotypes are often so inaccurate, why do we even have them? There is evidence that stereotypes facilitate information processing. In one study, participants were shown a videotaped interaction of a couple having a birthday dinner (Cohen, 1981). Half of participants were told that the woman in the video was a librarian, while the other half were told that she was a waitress. There were two versions of the videos, each of which included a mix of both stereotypical librarian and waitress behaviors. For example, in one video, the couple had roast beef (consistent with the librarian stereotype) and beer (consistent with the waitress stereotype). In the other video, the couple had hamburgers (waitress) and wine (librarian). After watching the video, participants took a memory test: a third of them took it immediately, another third took it 4 days later, and the final third took it a week later.

Irrespective of which version of the videos participants watched and when the memory test was administered, participants were more likely to recall stereotype-consistent features than stereotype-inconsistent features (Figure 3–3). In other words, participants who thought they were watching a librarian tended to recall roast beef or wine, while those who thought they were watching a waitress tended to recall hamburgers or beer. These results show that having stereotypes serves as a sort of memory aid. However, the flipside is that we are likely to overlook things we do not expect for a given person. Having stereotypes can thus be thought of as good *and* bad. They allow us to process the complex social world more effectively, but they sometimes cause us to overlook an unexpected reality.

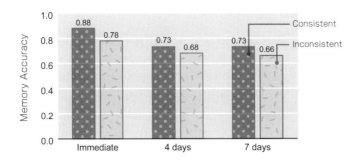

Figure 3-3. Memory accuracy as a function of stereotype consistency and delay. [Cohen, 1981 より筆者作成]

📖 **It is ～．That is ～の短縮形**　本書では堅苦しい表現を避けるために **It's** や **That's** という短縮形を使用している箇所があります。学術論文ではこのような短縮形を使わないのが一般的です。

Stereotype：ステレオタイプ　特定のグループの人たちに対する紋切り型の見方をステレオタイプといいます。

　本文の例で挙げているように，男性のほうが女性より背が高いという考えは，平均値レベルでは正しいものですが，個々の男女を比較したら必ずしもそうとはいえません。ステレオタイプは，ある特定のグループに対してひとつの特徴をあてはめるので（そしてグループの成員には常に個人差があるので），どうしても常に正しいというわけにはいきません。

　それとは別に，ステレオタイプの内容がそもそも間違っていることもあります。例えば，少数派のグループに対する差別的な信念（例えば，「彼らは生来の怠け者だ」「彼らは生まれつき知的に劣っている」といった信念）は多くの場合平均値レベルでも正しくありません。

　ステレオタイプは不正確だという話をするときには，平均値レベルでは正しいけれども個々の事例にあてはめると正しくないこともあるといっているのか，そもそもステレオタイプの内容が荒唐無稽であるといっているのか，よく考えて区別しないといけません。

1　この section では，「柔道」「九州男児」といった日本語の単語を英文中でローマ字表記し，斜体にしています。斜体にするのは強調のためではなく，外国語（もちろん英語話者にとってのです）の単語だということを示すためです。一方，下から 2 行目の good and bad の斜体は強調のための斜体です。

3.4 Illusory Correlation

Stereotypes guide our social cognition. We tend to see what we expect, and overlook the unexpected. This might seem a bit annoying, but surely it cannot cause too much trouble, can it? Regardless of the validity of a stereotype, because we naturally focus on confirmatory (i.e., stereotype-congruent) evidence, we come to increase our belief in the stereotype even if the stereotype, and the connections it asserts, are completely untenable. For example, although there is no established evidence for the relationship between ABO blood type and personality, many Japanese people still believe in this association. This typically involves selective perception: When you see someone who behaves in accord with a putative relationship, you think "Of course!" When you see someone who behaves in a contradictory manner, however, you simply ignore the person as an exception. In this way, we see a correlation between things that are not really related (i.e., an **illusory correlation**).

Illusory correlations can even occur when we have no prior expectation. This is because we associate rare events as occurring together. In an ingenious experiment conducted by Hamilton and Gifford (1976), participants viewed a series of slides, each of which described a person's behavior (e.g., John, a member of Group A, visited a sick friend in the hospital). As shown in Table 3-1, there are twice as many members of Group A as Group B. Also, there are more desirable than undesirable behaviors. However, it is important to notice that the frequency of undesirable behaviors is constant across the two groups (approximately 30% of the time). Nevertheless, participants were more likely to recall Group A members' desirable behaviors and Group B members' undesirable behaviors (Figure 3-4). Consequently, when asked about each group's impression, participants reported a significantly less favorable impression of Group B than of Group A. Of course, this relationship is illusory because there was no difference between group status and the frequency of undesirable behaviors (Table 3-1). The illusory correlation emerged simply because participants associated the two rare events (i.e., minority group membership and undesirable behaviors).

Once a group is associated with a characteristic, the stereotypical relationship may be further confirmed. In a related set of experiments, Hamilton and Rose (1980) presented participants with a series of cards, each describing a person's occupation (e.g., waitress, accountant) and traits (e.g., loud, mature). After examining all cards, participants attempted to recall the frequency that each trait word was presented with each occupation. Despite being equally likely to appear, participants recalled the stereotype-congruent combinations (be they positive or negative) more frequently than neutral or stereotype-incongruent combinations. If, therefore, you find yourself holding a stereotype (particularly a negative stereotype) about a group, perhaps you better think twice: the association may exist, but only in your head!

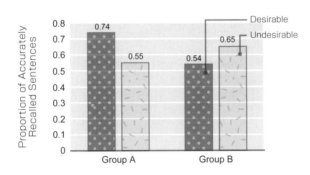

Table **3**-1. Distribution of stimulus sentences. Numbers in parentheses are the relative frequency of each type of behavior within each group. [Hamilton & Gifford, 1976]

Behavior	Group A	Group B
Desirable	18 (.69)	9 (.69)
Undesirable	8 (.31)	4 (.31)

この表は参加者に示されたスライドの内訳です。Group A の人が望ましい行動をしたスライドが 18 枚，Group B の人が望ましい行動をしたスライドが 9 枚あったというふうに見てください。

Figure **3**-4. Proportion of accurately recalled sentences within each stimulus type. [Hamilton & Gifford, 1976 より筆者作成]

Illusory Correlation：錯誤相関　統計的には関係のないもの同士に誤って関連があると思ってしまう現象のことを錯誤相関といいます。

　本文を読んでいて，もし社会的に望ましい行いのほうが珍しかったらどうなるのかと思われた読者もあるかもしれません。Hamilton & Gifford (1976) はもう 1 つ別の実験を行い，望ましい行動が少なく・望ましくない行動が多い状況での錯誤相関を検討しました（Table 3-1 の上下を逆転したような実験です）。その結果，少数派のほうがむしろ望ましいと見なされました。

3.5 Heuristics and Cognitive Biases

Heuristics are mental shortcuts, cognitive "rules-of-thumb." They allow people to make quick decisions based upon available information. Importantly, they reduce the cognitive load involved in decision making. However, as a tradeoff for their speed, many heuristics lead us to be inaccurate, causing us to commit errors known as **cognitive biases**. The following is a list of some common heuristics and cognitive biases that have the potential to affect social cognition (Tversky & Kahneman, 1974).

Availability Heuristic: We tend to use information that is *readily available to us* to make judgements, even when it is inappropriate to use it. For example, exposure to sensational reports of a terrible disease (e.g., cholera) leads us to overestimate the likelihood that we will be killed by this particular disease and leads to a number of biases.

Representativeness Heuristic: When we think about a group of events (or people), we tend to see salient characteristics as being representative of the group, which then influences our judgments.

Gambler's Fallacy: Even though the odds are equal that an event will occur (e.g., have a male or female child), after a long string of the event occurring one way (e.g., already having three girls), we expect that it is more likely to occur the other way (e.g., a baby boy will arrive). This is because alternating events (e.g., girl, boy, girl...) fit our image of randomness.

Base Rate Fallacy: Imagine that there are 30 engineers and 70 lawyers. One of them, Jack, has no interest in political issues, and his hobbies include mathematical puzzles. Guess the likelihood that Jack is an engineer. It seems pretty likely, right? However, did you pay any attention to the base rate (i.e., the likelihood of being an engineer is just 30%)? Kahneman and Tversky (1973) showed that people pay little attention to the base rate—in fact, reversing it (i.e., saying there were 70 engineers and 30 lawyers) makes virtually no difference in participants' estimates.

Conjunction Fallacy: Imagine a female philosophy major, Linda, who was deeply concerned with issues of discrimination when she was a student. What is the likelihood that she is a bank teller now? What is the likelihood that she is a bank teller *and* is active in the feminist movement? People tend to judge the latter likelihood to be greater than the former, although the latter is a part (i.e., a more detailed version) of the former (Tversky & Kahneman, 1983).

Anchoring and Adjustment Heuristic: In making numerical estimates, it is reasonable to start from some initial value, and adjust from it. However, adjustments are often insufficient. Guess (not compute) the product of $1 \times 2 \times 3 \times 4 \times 5 \times 6 \times 7 \times 8$ and the product of $8 \times 7 \times 6 \times 5 \times 4 \times 3 \times 2 \times 1$. Did you arrive at the same answer?

Heuristics：ヒューリスティック（ス）　複雑な問題を解くときに，時間をかけて確実に正解を導くかわりに用いられる素早く簡単な問題解決方法のことをヒューリスティックといいます。つまり，ヒューリスティックを用いれば，認知的負荷（cognitive load）を軽減することができます。ただし，簡便な解決法なので必ず正解に到達できるとは限りません。

　Tversky & Kahneman（1974）の論文で**利用可能性**（**availability**），**代表性**（**representativeness**），**係留と調整**（**anchoring and adjustment**）という3つのヒューリスティックが紹介されたため，これら3つについて述べるときには複数形の heuristics と表記されます。これに合わせても日本語でもヒューリスティックスと表記されていることがあります。

　後の論文で想像しやすいこと（頭の中でシミュレートしやすいこと）は起こりやすいと考えられやすいことが，シミュレーション・ヒューリスティックとして追加されました。例えば，ギリギリで電車に乗り遅れたら，大幅に遅刻して乗れなかったときよりも悔しいのではないでしょうか。これは，あのときこうしていたら乗れたのにという想像のしやすさの違いと説明されます。

Cognitive Bias：認知バイアス　Section 3.1 でも説明したように，バイアスは系統性をもった偏りという意味です。したがって，認知バイアスは，認知判断が規則性をもって真の値からずれることを意味します。

Gambler's Fallacy：ギャンブラーの錯誤

Base Rate Fallacy：基準率無視

Conjunction Fallacy：連言錯誤

補足1　利用可能性ヒューリスティックの例としてよく挙げられるのは，英単語でrで始まる単語の数はrが3番目にくる単語よりも多く見積もられやすいというものです。最初にrで始まる単語は思いつきやすいですが，3番目といわれるとなかなか思いつきません。ですが，よく考えると car, dark, personal などたくさんあって，実際には3番目にrがつく単語のほうがたくさんあります。

　ランダム性についての誤解はギャンブラーの錯誤（gambler's fallacy）以外にもたくさんあります。例えば，飛行機事故が何件か続くと何か関連があるのではないかと思いがちです。しかし，本当のランダム事象は私たちが思っている以上に，何もない時期があった後に事件が立て続けに起こるというような結果になりがちなのです。

Advanced Topic: The Accuracy of Social Cognition

Throughout this chapter, we have emphasized that people are prone to make mistakes. Admitting *"to err is human"* wholeheartedly, perhaps we have conveyed a too-pessimistic view of social cognition—our understandings of the social world may appear hopelessly inaccurate and unreliable. To hold this impression, however, would be misguided. Here, we focus on one of the few articles that report on accurate social cognition.

As a background for this research, however, we must present one last cognitive bias—the **false consensus effect**. People tend to (falsely) assume that their own attitudes and beliefs are close to attitude and beliefs held by the majority of other people. In a famous experiment, Ross, Greene, and House (1977) asked participants to wear a sandwich board, which said either "Eat at Joe's" or "Repent," and walk through a university campus for 30 minutes. Researchers alleged that the aim of the study was to investigate how other students would respond to the sign on the board. Participants were then told that they could quit this study if they did not want to wear the board. In total, 48 participants (60%) decided to continue the study, while 32 participants (40%) decided to quit the study. They were then asked to estimate what proportion of their fellow students would agree to carry the board. Those who decided to continue the study estimated 62% of fellow students would do so, while those who decided to quit the study estimated that 77% of fellow students would refuse to carry the board. Clearly, participants believed that their own choice (regardless of its actual likelihood) would be shared by the majority of their fellow students.

Two social psychologists, Nisbett and Kunda (1985), took a new approach to a similar problem, but reached a different conclusion. A first set of participants were asked to indicate their own attitudes on various issues (e.g., How do you feel about people of your own age taking hard drugs?) with either a 9-point or 5-point scale. A second set of participants were asked to estimate the distributions of 100 fellow students' responses using the same scale. Do you think the estimated distributions were drastically different from the actual distributions? If your answer is YES, you are mistaken! As shown in Figure 3-5, the actual and estimated distributions were remarkably similar. It is true that participants' differences in inaccuracies canceled each other out. It is also true that some common biases (e.g., the false consensus effect) were observed in this study as well. Even taking these issues into account, the similarity between the actual and estimated distributions is impressive, isn't it? A take-home message is obvious: social cognition must be at least partially accurate, for if there were no accuracy at all, how could we be systematically biased against it?

Figure 3-5

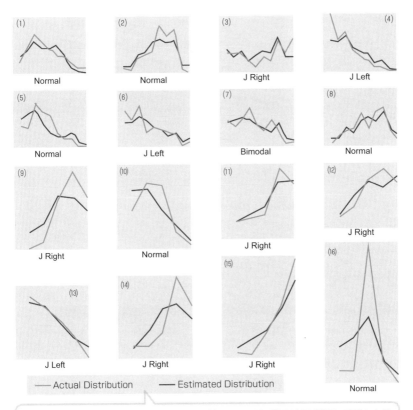

Nisbett & Kunda (1985)で用いられた質問の例（これら以外の質問は次頁「補足」で紹介します）
(3) How do you feel about women being allowed to have an abortion on demand?
(6) How do you feel about increasing defense spending?
(8) How do you feel about people your age living with another person while not being married?

*
Actual distributionと書かれた灰色のラインは，実際の参加者の意見がどのように分布していたかを示しています。一方，estimated distributionと書かれた黒いラインは，別の参加者が予測した意見分布を示しています。この2つの分布はどのような内容の質問かによらずよく似ています。つまり人々は，さまざまなことがらに対する意見がどのように分布しているかをある程度正確に把握しているということです。

Figure 3-5. Actual and estimated distributions for 16 attitudinal items. The letters below each figure denote the shape of the actual distribution (Normal = normal distribution; J Right = J-shape with central tendency on the extreme right side; J Left = J-shape with central tendency on the extreme left side; Bimodal = bimodal distribution). [Nisbett & Kunda, 1985]

False Consensus Effect：フォールス・コンセンサス効果（「誤った合意性推論」と訳されることもあります）

References

Cohen, C. E. (1981). Person categories and social perception: Testing some boundaries of the processing effect of prior knowledge. *Journal of Personality and Social Psychology, 40*, 441-452. doi: 10.1037/0022-3514.40.3.441

Hamilton, D. L., & Gifford, R. K. (1976). Illusory correlation in interpersonal perception: A cognitive basis of stereotypic judgments. *Journal of Experimental Social Psychology, 12*, 392-407. doi: 10.1016/S0022-1031(76)80006-6

Hamilton, D. L., & Rose, T. L. (1980). Illusory correlation and the maintenance of stereotypic beliefs. *Journal of Personality and Social Psychology, 39*, 832-845. doi: 10.1037/0022-3514.39.5.832

Heider, F. (1958). *The psychology of interpersonal relations.* New York: John Wiley & Sons.

Jones, E. E., & Harris, V. A. (1967). The attribution of attitudes. *Journal of Experimental Social Psychology, 3*, 1-24. doi: 10.1016/0022-1031(67)90034-0

Kahneman, D., & Tversky, A. (1973). On the psychology of prediction. *Psychological Review, 80*, 237-251. doi: 10.1037/h0034747

Kunda, Z. (1987). Motivated inference: Self-serving generation and evaluation of causal theories. *Journal of Personality and Social Psychology, 53*, 636-647. doi: 10.1037/0022-3514.53.4.636

Nisbett, R. E., & Kunda, Z. (1985). Perception of social distributions. *Journal of Personality and Social Psychology, 48*, 297-311. doi: 10.1037/0022-3514.48.2.297

Ross, L., Greene, D., & House, P. (1977). The "false consensus effect": An egocentric bias in social perception and attribution processes. *Journal of Experimental Social Psychology, 13*, 279-301. doi: 10.1016/0022-1031(77)90049-X

Tversky, A., & Kahneman, D. (1974). Judgment under uncertainty: Heuristics and biases. *Science, 185*, 1124-1131. doi: 10.1126/science.185.4157.1124

Tversky, A., & Kahneman, D. (1983). Extensional versus intuitive reasoning: The conjunction fallacy in probability judgment. *Psychological Review, 90*, 293-315. doi: 10.1037/0033-295X.90.4.293

補足2　Figure 3-5 の Nisbett & Kunda（1985）の研究で用いられた質問の例

Items measured by a 9-point scale (1 = very strongly disapprove − 9 = very strongly approve)：(1) How do you feel about the University's plan to eliminate some schools and departments in order to generate money for new programs? (2) How do you feel about Harold Shapiro's conduct of the University Presidency to date? (4) How do you feel about people your own age taking hard drugs? (5) How do you feel about U.S. intervention to support the government in El Salvador? (7) How do you feel about Ronald Reagan's conduct of the Presidency to date?

Items measured by a 5-point scale (1 = dislike very much − 5 = like very much)：(9) the television anchor Dan Rather, (10) international oil companies, (11) McDonald's hamburgers, (12) the actress Jane Fonda, (13) the Moral Majority, (14) Campbell's chicken noodle soup, (15) the movie Star Wars, (16) Saudi Arabians.

CHAPTER 4

Impression Formation and Interpersonal Attraction

印象形成と対人魅力

4.1
Forming Impressions of Others

4.2
"Diagnosticity" of Social Information

4.3
Proximity and the Mere Exposure Effect

4.4
Do Birds of a Feather Really Flock Together?

4.5
The Effect of Physical Attractiveness

4.1 Forming Impressions of Others

Impression formation (i.e., how we form impressions of others) is one of the classic social psychology research topics. As early as 1946, Asch published an article entitled "Forming Impressions of Personality," in which he proposed a distinction between **central traits** and **peripheral traits**: Certain characteristics are of more central importance to forming an impression than other, less important, more peripheral characteristics.

Asch provided participants with either one of two lists of personality characteristics and tasked his participants with forming an impression of a target person. List A included the items "intelligent, skillful, industrious, *warm*, determined, practical, [and] cautious," while List B included the same items but replaced the item *warm* with *cold*. Although the two lists differed only in terms of the fourth trait (warm or cold), participants formed drastically different impressions of the two targets (see the following page for sample excerpts from participants' reports). Those participants who received List A considered the target more favorable in terms of a number of characteristics such as generosity, sociability, popularity, imaginativeness, and sense of humor. When Asch replaced the critical, central traits (warm and cold) with less central, more peripheral, traits (polite and blunt), participants formed nearly identical impressions.

Kelley (1950) tested Asch's findings in a face-to-face setting. He introduced a class discussion leader as either a warm or cold person, along with other background information. The discussion leader and participants (half of whom were told he was a "warm" person, and half of whom were told he was "cold") then engaged in a 20-minute group discussion. Kelley essentially replicated Asch's results. Participants who expected the discussion leader to be a cold person formed a less favorable impression than participants who expected him to be a warm person. It is worth remembering that participants were in the same group discussion, and thus saw the same person behave in the exact same manner. Nevertheless, participants in the cold condition perceived the discussion leader as being more self-centered, formal, unsociable, unpopular, irritable, humorless, and ruthless than those in the warm condition. Concordant with these impressions, in the cold condition, only 32% of participants actually took part in the discussion, compared with more than half (56%) who engaged in the discussion in the warm condition.

Starting with these seminal studies, social psychology has accumulated a large body of knowledge about how people form impressions of others and what traits people seek in their relationship partners. In this chapter, we will look at what happens in our minds when we meet new people, as well as some social psychological factors that help explain the genesis of friendships and romantic relationships.

Impression Formation：印象形成　　私たちが他者に対して特定の印象をもつことを印象形成といいます。

　英語では，impression の前に my や your のような所有格があれば印象を抱いている人のことを意味します。それに対して，impression of O となっているときには，O は印象をもたれている対象のことです。例えば，my impression of you というと「私があなたに対して抱いている印象」ということになります。O が物であれば混乱はありませんが，O が人のときには混乱しないように注意してください。

Central Traits/Peripheral Traits：中心特性／周辺特性　　Asch（1946）は印象形成に大きな影響をもつ特性とそうでない特性があることに気づき，大きな影響をもつ特性を中心特性，さほど大きな影響をもたない特性を周辺特性と呼びました。

補足 3　Asch の実験の参加者が報告した印象の例（Asch, 1946, p. 246）

- List A を提示された人が抱いた印象の例：A person who believes certain things to be right, wants others to see his point, would be sincere in an argument and would like to see his point won.
- List B を提示された人が抱いた印象の例：A rather snobbish person who feels that his success and intelligence set him apart from the run-of-the-mill individual. Calculating and unsympathetic.

4.2 "Diagnosticity" of Social Information

As we saw in the previous section, Asch (1946), who was a major proponent of Gestalt ("Holistic") social psychology, took an all-at-once approach to impression formation. Proposing **information integration theory**, Anderson (1981), by contrast, brought focus to the piecemeal (i.e., step-by-step) side of impression formation. This approach revealed a number of interesting features of impression formation, including **negativity bias**: When we are given the same number of both positive and negative pieces of information about a target person, we tend to form a slightly negative impression.

Skowronski and Carlston (1987) argued that negativity bias arises because people generally perceive negative information (e.g., person A "cheated at poker") as more diagnostic about a target person's personality than positive information (e.g., person A "worked hard when the boss was away"). You might suspect that the target person performed the positive behavior (e.g., worked hard) because he or she was afraid that someone might be monitoring him or her. In this way, we are likely to discount the diagnostic value (or **diagnosticity**) of positive information. On the other hand, you might expect that someone who cheats at poker is likely to cheat in different situations. In light of this asymmetry, knowing the same number of positive and negative pieces of information results in a relatively negative impression of a target person.

Nevertheless, Skowronski and Carlston noticed that people tend to treat negative information about ability (e.g., person A "bought himself clothes that were the wrong size") quite differently from negative information about morality (e.g., person A "wrote a bad check"). In the case of ability, the researchers surmised that people would be more forgiving of negative information when forming an impression. That is, they predicted a positivity bias in the ability domain.

To test these seemingly contradictory hypotheses, the researchers examined impressions formed based on two pieces of information from the abovementioned domains. They employed a 2 (domain: morality or ability) × 5 (cue 1 value: extremely positive, positive, neutral, negative, or extremely negative) × 5 (cue 2 value) **factorial design**, with the domain factor as a **between-participants** condition, and the two cue factors acting as **repeated measures**. Results are shown in Figures 4-1a (morality) and 4-1b (ability). The horizontal axis represents the cue value of the first piece of information, the different lines represent the cue value of the second piece of information, and the vertical axis represents the impression of the target person. As expected, a single negative or extremely negative cue in the morality domain was much more damaging than in the ability domain, where by contrast, our impressions of others tend to be more concerned with cues of positive information.

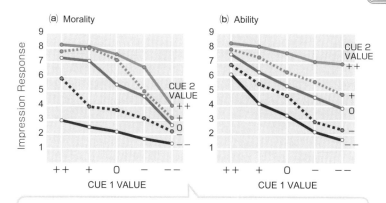

この図では5通りの cue value が、それぞれ++ (extremely positive), + (positive), 0 (neutral), − (negative), −− (extremely negative) と表記されています。左側の(a)では1つ目の cue value が−−だと2つ目の cue value によらず印象がおしなべて悪くなっています。これをもってネガティヴィティ・バイアスの証拠と考えます。

Figure **4**-1. Impression as a function of two cue values in the domains of (a) morality and (b) ability. [Skowronski & Carlston, 1987]

Information Integration Theory：情報統合理論　　人々が多くの手がかり（cue）をどのように統合し、最終的な社会的判断を下すかをモデル化することを目指す情報処理のモデルです。モデルの検討として、複数の手がかりを実験参加者に与えて、彼らが下す社会的判断を調べます。

　例えば、ある特性についての判断（診断）に役にたつ程度（**diagnosticity**）が+1の情報（ほどほどよい情報）と−1の情報（ほどほど悪い情報）を与えるとします。情報が等しく重み付けられて平均されるなら印象は0（よくも悪くもない）です。ところが、この場合に報告される印象が悪いものであればネガティヴな情報が印象形成でより影響力をもつ、つまりネガティヴィティ・バイアス（**negativity bias**）があるということになります。

📖 実験のデザイン（要因計画）について　　実験では参加者を無作為に2つの条件に割り振ることがあります。実験の基本的な考え方ですが、これを参加者間要因配置（**between-participants factorial design**）の実験といいます。このデザインは、ひとつの条件で実験に参加することでもうひとつの条件での反応に強い影響が出るときに有効です。これに対して、この実験では5×5の25種類の情報の組み合わせについて印象を尋ねても、反応に大きな影響がでないと考えて、各参加者に25種類すべてについて印象を回答してもらっています。これを参加者内要因配置（**within-participant factorial design**）または反復測定（**repeated measures**）といいます。参加者間要因配置の場合、一般に between-participants と participant を複数形にするので注意してください。

CHAPTER **4**　Impression Formation and Interpersonal Attraction

4.3 Proximity and the Mere Exposure Effect

Did you have any friends in your childhood neighborhood? Most likely your answer is YES. But can you explain why? Maybe, you went to the same kindergarten or elementary school, or perhaps you played together on weekends. You may have been in the same club or on the same sporting team. These obvious conditions aside, there must be other reasons for your friendship. Right?

Around the middle of the twentieth century, three social psychologists, Festinger, Schachter, and Back (1950), conducted a field study at two dormitory buildings at the Massachusetts Institute of Technology (MIT). The psychologists were interested in the social dynamics of the residents of the two aforementioned buildings, and discovered that **proximity** (also known by the formal term, **propinquity**, in older texts) is an important factor in friendship formation. Residents were more likely to become friends with someone next door than with someone at the other end of the same floor. Furthermore, when physical distance is the same, so-called *functional distance* (e.g., whether residents used the same stairway of the building) becomes important.

Festinger et al. (1950) surmised that frequent contacts (mostly passive contacts) facilitate friendship formation. This effect of passive contact is now known as the **mere exposure effect** (Zajonc, 1968). Zajonc presented a series of photographs of men's faces to his participants, who were led to believe that they were taking part in a visual memory study. The photos were presented for 2 seconds each. Unbeknownst to participants, each photo was presented either once, twice, five times, ten times, or twenty five times. After this serial presentation session, participants were asked how much they liked each of the photos, along with new photos that had never been presented. Zajonc's results are shown in Figure 4-2. Consistent with Festinger et al.'s interpretation of the effect of proximity, the more frequently participants saw a man's face, the more they liked him.

Later studies have revealed that even **unconscious** exposure to stimuli yields the mere exposure effect. If faces were presented to you very quickly (e.g., for 5 milliseconds), you could not consciously perceive them. If asked, you would say "they are new to me." Nevertheless, liking faces increases as the frequency of unconscious exposure increases (e.g., Bornstein & D'Agostino, 1992).

Your neighbors, by dictionary definition, are those people that live in close proximity to you; you are exposed to them more frequently than people who are not your neighbors. In the end, neighbors often become friends. According to the above studies, two mutually related factors over which we have little control, proximity and mere exposure, may explain a large portion of our fondness for some individuals over others.

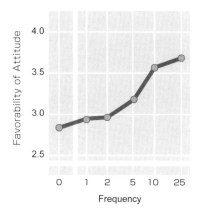

Figure 4-2. Liking of the photographs as a function of frequency of exposure. [Zajonc, 1968]

Proximity（Propinquity）：近接性　　近接性は対象と近くにいるということです。
　Festinger らの研究で示されたことは，近くに住んでいるというだけで（近接性が高いだけで）相手に対して好意をもちやすいということです。

Mere Exposure Effect：単純接触効果　　単純接触効果は，人に対する好意だけでなく，無意味な単語や図形にもあてはまります。
　この効果を報告した Zajonc という研究者はポーランドの出身で，ザイアンスと読みます。この他にも社会的促進に関する研究（CHAPTER 7）など多くの古典的な研究で有名な社会心理学者です。そのため，教科書などでよく目にしますが，そのままではなかなか正しく読めない名前なので紹介しておきます。

📖 **Unconsciousness：無意識または非意識**　　現代の心理学でいう無意識とは，刺激が目の前に提示されても呈示時間が短かすぎるなどの理由で意識の上にのぼらないことをいいます。Sigmund Freud（フロイト）が精神分析で唱えた無意識とは意味合いが違うので，そのことをあえて強調するために nonconsciousness（非意識）と書かれていることもあります。

CHAPTER 4　Impression Formation and Interpersonal Attraction

4.4 Do Birds of a Feather Really Flock Together?

An old English adage, much like its Japanese counterpart, says that "birds of a feather flock together[1]." However, is this really so? This question was experimentally tackled by Byrne and Nelson (1965). They tested whether **similarity** really fosters interpersonal attraction by having participants fill out an attitude questionnaire, which measured attitudes toward various random topics, such as science fiction, welfare legislation, gardening, etc. Employing **deception**, Byrne and Nelson explained that the experiment was about the accuracy of interpersonal judgments based on limited information. Participants then received a questionnaire allegedly filled out by someone else. The bogus answers were either similar or dissimilar to the participants' own answers. Participants then rated the interpersonal attractiveness of the target person. Figure 4-3 shows the combined results of Byrne's studies (reported in Byrne & Nelson, 1965). As the small triangles show, as similarity with the target (represented on the horizontal axis) increases, favorable attitudes toward the target (represented on the vertical axis) also increase. The upward straight line is a statistically derived line that best fits the data (i.e., the triangles)

This effect of similarity was explained as a sort of **reinforcement**. If your partner shares many attitudes with you, you feel validated when interacting with your partner; in this way, interaction with your (similar) partner provides psychological rewards. Notice that the same is also true for your partner. Therefore, the similarity effect might also be connected to another well-studied factor of liking—someone else's liking for you: if you know that a person likes you, you also tend to like that person. This phenomenon is called **reciprocity of liking** or **reciprocal liking**.

In one illustrative experiment (Backman & Secord, 1959), participants engaged in a series of tasks (e.g., personality tests) with a group of nine fellow same-sex students. The experimenter then bogusly informed participants that certain group members would probably be fond of them based upon their personality tests. Finally, after joining in a brief self-introduction session, participants were asked to nominate who they liked. Consistent with the theory of reciprocal liking, participants tended to nominate the group members who they had been (falsely) informed would like them.

The effects of similarity and reciprocity may go hand in hand. Imagine that person (A) shares a hobby with another person (B). A's impression of B is favorable due to the similarity effect. Importantly, B's impression of A is probably favorable, again due to the similarity effect. This in turn fosters A's liking of B due to reciprocity of liking. Thus, similarity not only fosters liking, but may also ignite the reciprocity process. Moreover, these effects are bi-directional—the same events may occur for B as well!

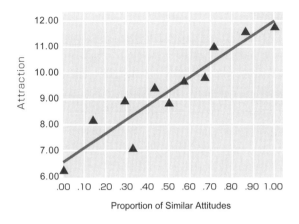

Figure **4**-3. The relationship between the proportion of similar attitudes and attraction. [Byrne & Nelson, 1965]

Similarity：類似性　　相手との態度や性格が似ていることです。態度以外にも性格などいろいろな面で似ているということがありますが，社会心理学で特に研究されてきたのは態度の類似性です。

Deception：ディセプション　　本当の目的がわかってしまうと正直な反応を見ることができないときに，実験の参加者に本来とは違った目的や実験状況の説明をすることがあります。参加者を騙すことになるので，欺瞞的な手続き（deceptive procedure）ということになります。カタカナでディセプションといっています。

Reinforcement：強化

Reciprocity of Liking（**Reciprocal Liking**）：好意の返報性　　Reciprocity は互恵性と訳されることもあります（特に，自分に親切にしてくれた相手に親切を返すときには互恵性という訳語が使われることがあります）。ですが，好意については返報性を使うのが一般的です。

1　Birds of a feather flock together：類は友を呼ぶ

CHAPTER **4**　Impression Formation and Interpersonal Attraction

4.5 The Effect of Physical Attractiveness

Have you ever thought that the principle of similarity might extend to **physical attractiveness**, that more attractive men date more attractive women, and pairs like *Beauty and the Beast*[1] are rare in real life? This is known as the **matching hypothesis**, and it predicts assortment of couples in terms of their physical attractiveness.

The first experiment that attempted to test the matching hypothesis was conducted by Hatfield (at the time, Walster) and her colleagues (Walster, Aronson, Abrahams, & Rottman, 1966). They invited university freshmen to attend a "Computer Dance" event, scheduled at the end of freshman orientation week, by purporting that a new technology would match each participant with his or her perfect date. Thus, around the beginning of orientation week, each participant filled out a personality test which was apparently fed into a computer program. In fact, at this point, experimental assistants secretly assessed everyone's physical attractiveness. According to this assessment, participants were divided into three levels of attractiveness (high, middle, or low).

At the dance, people were semi-randomly matched (males were not matched with females taller than themselves). Thus, each pair was assigned to one of 3 (male attractiveness) × 3 (female attractiveness) conditions. At the end of the dance, participants answered how much they liked their partner. Contrary to Walster et al.'s prediction from the matching hypothesis (i.e., high attractiveness people prefer each other, middles prefer middles, and the lows the lows) they found that irrespective of gender and own level of attractiveness, participants liked physically attractive partners more than less physically attractive partners (see Figure 4-4). Moreover, male participants who had been matched with physically attractive partners were more likely to ask their partners out on a date.

Walster et al.'s finding might first appear contradictory to a common observation—real married couples tend to have similar levels of physical attractiveness. However, preference at the individual level (i.e., always date someone prettier) does not necessarily correspond with the aggregated phenomenon (i.e., couples tend to be similar in attractiveness). Even though each individual tries to maximize his or her partner's attractiveness, the resultant couples end up seeming to confirm the matching hypothesis. Why? This is easily demonstrated by a simple pairing game (Ellis & Kelley, 1999).

Put a randomly chosen number on participants' foreheads so that they cannot see their own number. Then, ask them to try to pair off with another participant. Each participant will receive some rewards (e.g., money, credits) according to the number on their partner's forehead. Participants naturally seek out a high-number partner to maximize their rewards. If you have a low number, sorry—you will be rejected many times. The highest individuals tend to form pairs first, the second-highest individuals next, and so on!

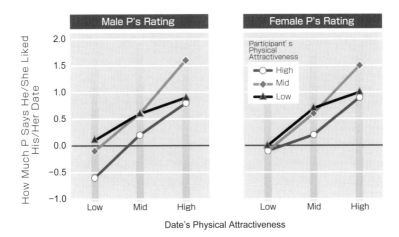

Figure 4-4. Average liking of one's partner as a function of one's own level of attractiveness and the partner's level of attractiveness. ［Walster et al., 1966 より筆者作成］

Physical Attractiveness：身体的魅力度　魅力度という言葉に身体的という形容詞がついたこの用語は，外見のよさだけを指しています。あえて身体的魅力度と魅力度（attractiveness）を使い分けている論文があったら，後者は内面的な魅力度などを総合したものを指して使われていると考えてください。

Matching Hypothesis：つり合い仮説　つり合い仮説とは，私たちが自分と魅力度の似た相手を求めるという仮説です。実際のカップルの魅力度がつり合っていることが多いという観察に基づいて提唱されました。

　本文でも述べているように，つり合い仮説を個人の好みの問題として考えるとすれば，間違っています。各個人は単にできるだけ魅力的な相手とつき合いたいと思っているのです。ところが，全員がこのように思っていると，魅力的でない人が魅力的な相手に交際を申し込んでも断られるので，できあがるカップルはだいたい魅力度がつり合った者同士ということになります。

　本文では簡単なデモンストレーション用のゲーム（pairing game）を紹介しています（これは20人程度の教室であれば簡単に実施できます）。もっと厳密にこの問題を知りたければ，コンピュータ・シミュレーションで詳しく検討した研究もあります（Kalick & Hamilton, 1986）。

1　*Beauty and the Beast*：邦題『美女と野獣』　ディズニーの映画でよく知られていますが，もとはフランスのおとぎ話です。

References

Anderson, N. H. (1981). *Foundation of information integration theory*. New York: Academic Press.

Asch, S. E. (1946). Forming impressions of personality. *Journal of Abnormal and Social Psychology, 41*, 258-290. doi: 10.1037/h0055756

Backman, C. W., & Secord, P. F. (1959). The Effect of perceived liking on interpersonal attraction. *Human Relations, 12*, 379-384. doi: 10.1177/001872675901200407

Bornstein, R. F., & D'Agostino, P. R. (1992). Stimulus recognition and the mere exposure effect. *Journal of Personality and Social Psychology, 63*, 545-552. doi: 10.1037/0022-3514.63.4.545

Byrne, D., & Nelson, D. (1965). Attraction as a linear function of proportion of positive reinforcements. *Journal of Personality and Social Psychology, 1*, 659-663. doi: 10.1037/h0022073

Ellis, B., & Kelley, H. H. (1999). The pairing game: A classroom demonstration of the matching phenomenon. *Teaching of Psychology, 26*, 118-121. doi: 10.1207/s15328023top2602_8

Festinger, L., Schachter, S., & Back, K. (1950). *Social pressures in informal groups*. New York: Harper.

Kalick, S. M., & Hamilton, T. E. (1986). The matching hypothesis reexamined. *Journal of Personality and Social Psychology, 51*, 673-682. doi: 10.1037/0022-3514.51.4.673

Kelley, H. H. (1950). The warm-cold variable in first impressions of persons. *Journal of Personality, 18*, 431-439. doi: 10.1111/j.1467-6494.1950.tb01260.x

Skowronski, J. J., & Carlston, D. E. (1987). Social judgment and social memory: The role of cue diagnosticity in negativity, positivity, and extremity biases. *Journal of Personality and Social Psychology, 52*, 689-699. doi: 10.1037/0022-3514.52.4.689

Walster, E., Aronson, V., Abrahams, D., & Rottman, L. (1966). Importance of physical attractiveness in dating behavior. *Journal of Personality and Social Psychology, 4*, 508-516. doi: 10.1037/h0021188

Zajonc, R. B. (1968). Attitudinal effects of mere exposure. *Journal of Personality and Social Psychology, 9*, 1-27. doi: 10.1037/h0025848

CHAPTER

Emotions

感情・情動

5.1
Affect, Emotion, and Mood

5.2
The Role of Bodily Feedback: The James-Lange Theory

5.3
The Role of Interpretation: The Two-Factor Theory

5.4
Do Emotions Require Cognition?

5.5
Basic Emotions and Facial Expressions

5.1 Affect, Emotion, and Mood

Have you seen the 2015 Disney/Pixar film, *Inside Out*[1]? The audience is introduced to five distinct emotions (Joy, Sadness, Anger, Fear, and Disgust) who live inside the head of a little girl named Riley. They guide her every move, sometimes alone, making her laugh or causing her anger, and sometimes together, as when Joy and Sadness team up to give Riley tears of joy. The film's naïve characterization of emotions—*inner* feelings that guide our behavior—corresponds well with the etymology[2] of emotion: something that *moves* (Latin: *movere* ⇨ *motion*) a person outward (Latin: *ex* ⇨ *e*). It also corresponds rather well with the current, scientific understanding of emotion.

As a first step to thinking about emotion, it is important to precisely define the term. Unfortunately, there is no consensus over what an emotion actually is! To make things worse, the distinction between emotion and related terms, such as affect and mood, is often ambiguous. So, in an attempt to prevent further confusion, here we offer a relatively widely accepted view. The term "**affect**" is generally considered a larger category encompassing both "**emotion**" and "**mood**." Emotions are elicited by some obvious cause, and entail strong subjective feelings that are relatively short-lived. Moods, on the other hand, are not necessarily elicited by an obvious cause, and entail only subtle feelings that can last for a very long time, days or even weeks. There are various types of emotions, while moods are typically only positive or negative.

In this chapter, we mostly focus on emotions. We are afraid that we might give you an impression that moods, weak and subtle affects, are unimportant, especially compared to strong, "moving," emotions. However, moods are important, too. To compensate, here we present a phenomenon related to mood, the **mood congruence effect**: People are more likely to recall events that match the positivity or negativity of their mood.

In one study, Bower (1981) asked participants to keep a diary of emotional events for a week. Parenthetically, participants recorded more pleasant than unpleasant events: on average twice as many pleasant events as unpleasant events were reported in their diaries (maybe due to *positive illusions*: Section 2.3). A week later, participants took part in a recall session. Participants were first put in either a positive or negative mood via hypnosis. They then tried to recall the events in their diaries as much as possible. As shown in Figure 5-1, participants in a positive mood recalled more pleasant events from their diaries, while those in a negative mood recalled more unpleasant events. The mood congruence effect is an instance of an affect-cognition interaction.

All things considered, emotions remain something of an enigma. Here, we present a brief historical overview of emotion research, so that you will be prepared to explore this enigma by yourself.

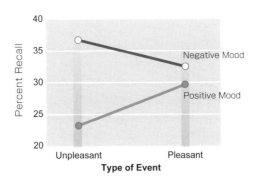

Figure 5-1. Percentage of recall from daily diaries as a function of current mood and the pleasantness of events. [Bower, 1981]

Affect, Emotion, and Mood：感情・情動・気分　辞書を引くとaffectにもemotionにも「**感情**」という訳語が書かれていますが，心理学では（特にaffectと区別するときには）emotionに「**情動**」という言葉があてられます。ただし，emotionを感情と訳している教科書などもあるので注意してください。

Affect 感情	Emotion 情動	Obvious Cause Strong Short-Lived
	Mood 気分	Cause Not Necessarily Known Weak Long-Lasting

Mood Congruence Effect：気分一致効果　そのときの気分（ムード）にあった過去の経験を思い出しやすいことを気分一致効果といいます。よい気分のときにはよいこと，悪い気分のときには悪いことを思い出しやすいということです。

1　*Inside Out*：邦題『インサイド・ヘッド』
2　Etymology：語源学（語源の説明）

5.2 The Role of Bodily Feedback: The James-Lange Theory

In the late 19th century, William James pondered about what an emotion really is (the same James who famously distinguished *Me-* and *I*-selves: Section 2.1). His primary concern regarded the timing of emotional processes—which comes first, subjective feelings or bodily reactions? "Common sense says, we lose our fortune, are sorry and weep; we meet a bear, are frightened and run..." wrote James (1884, p. 190). However after careful analysis, James thought it best to refute common sense, "the more rational statement is that we feel sorry because we cry" and "[we feel] afraid because we tremble."

According to James, first we encounter a stimulus or event (e.g., a bear). Next, we experience physiological changes consistent with the event (e.g., trembling, an elevated heart rate, a fearful facial expression, etc.). It is only *after* these physiological changes that we experience the emotion (e.g., "I'm so scared!"). The logic behind this theory is that physiological changes in our body act as a source of information (i.e., bodily feedback) that our brain uses to inform us of our emotional states. Shortly after James published this feedback theory, a contemporary physician, Carl Lange, arrived at a very similar conclusion. Therefore, the idea (i.e., bodily feedback creates emotional experience) became known, **eponymously**, as the **James-Lange theory**.

You might ask whether there is any evidence for such a counterintuitive theory, and you may be surprised to know that the answer is YES. In a simple and straightforward experiment, Strack, Martin, and Stepper (1988) examined whether people would evaluate cartoons as funnier when smiling, even when they were smiling for a completely unrelated reason. Participants thus were instructed to hold a pen with either their teeth, lips, or non-dominant hand. As you can see in Figure 5-2 (right), when they held the pen with their teeth, participants had to use muscles that they usually use to make a smile. By contrast, the lip instruction caused participants to use the muscles that they typically use to make a frown (Figure 5-2 left). The third instruction (i.e., the non-dominant hand instruction) served as a control condition. Under each of these instructions, participant read cartoons and evaluated each cartoon's funniness from 0 (*not at all funny*) to 9 (*very funny*).

In support of the central prediction of the James-Lange theory, as shown in Figure 5-3, participants rated the same cartoons as most funny in the teeth condition and least funny in the lip condition. The facial expressions of participants (i.e., the experimentally manipulated smiles and frowns) actually changed participants' feelings according to the usual valence of these expressions (positive vs. negative). Thus, when you are feeling sad, why not make a smile? It doesn't cost a thing, and it may actually make you feel better.

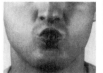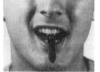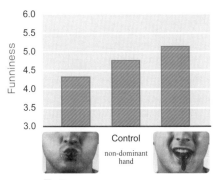

Figure **5**-2. Illustrative facial expressions yielded by the two pen-holding instructions, the lip condition (left) and the teeth condition (right). [Strack et al., 1988]

Figure **5**-3. Mean funniness rating as a function of the experimental condition. [Strack et al., 1988 より筆者作成]

📖 **Eponymous**　辞書的な訳語は「名祖（なおや）の」となっています。つまり，何かがある人物の名前にちなんで名づけられたということです。

(o)nym はギリシア語の name からきているので，名詞や名前に関連する言葉をつくります（これを -nymous にすると形容詞になります）。以下は論文などでもときどき見かけるものです。

例　　anonym　匿名　　　　anonymous　匿名の
　　　synonym　同義語　　　synonymous　同義の
　　　antonym　反意語　　　antonymous　反意語の
　　　acronym　頭文字を並べた略語（NATO, UNESCO 等）

英語で文章を書く場合で，ある単語を似たような意味の単語に言い換えたい，ある単語の反対の意味の単語が出てこないというようなときには，検索エンジンにその単語と一緒に synonym（または antonym）といれると，類義語辞典などのページが出てくるので便利です。

James-Lange Theory：**ジェームズ=ランゲ説**　　ジェームズ=ランゲ説の特徴は，身体の状態についての情報が脳にフィードバック（feedback）されることの役割を強調する点です。

5.3 The Role of Interpretation: The Two-Factor Theory

The James-Lange theory, which was the first scientific theory of emotion, emerged around the end of the 19th century. By the 1920s, a physiologist, Walter Cannon, mounted a criticism of the theory based on the latest findings of the time. Cannon argued that the autonomic nervous system[1] produces a rather uniform physiological reaction (**physiological arousal** under the influence of **epinephrine**) and that differentiated bodily feedbacks, which are key to the James-Lange theory, are impossible. Moreover, he argued that physiological arousal is too slow to serve as a useful source of information (e.g., taking just a second to feel fear in response to a bear could prove fatal). Cannon maintained that the brain (especially the **thalamus** and **hypothalamus**) produces emotions *before* physiological changes occur. This is called the **Cannon-Bard theory** after Cannon and his student, Philip Bard.

In 1962, on the heels of the "cognitive revolution," Schachter and Singer reexamined the uniformity of physiological arousal. If physiological states cannot tell us what emotion we should feel, something else has to do the work. They surmised that cognition does the job. According to their thesis, a stimulus first evokes physiological arousal. However, this is insufficient to produce an emotion—cognition is required to interpret the situation. This interpretation determines the meaning of the physiological arousal. Schachter and Singer's theory is often called the **two-factor theory of emotion**, as it assumes that both bodily arousal and cognition (interpretation) are necessary ingredients of emotion.

The two-factor theory makes an interesting prediction—misattributions should alter our subjective experiences of physiological arousal. Dutton and Aron (1974) tested this prediction with the help of... a river, the Capilano River in Vancouver, Canada, where there is a famous, rather scary, suspension bridge. It is pretty much impossible to cross the bridge without becoming physiologically aroused. Dutton and Aron examined whether misattribution of this arousal to a source other than the bridge would make a change in subjective experience.

The experiment employed a 2 (location: suspension bridge vs. solid bridge) × 2 (interviewer gender: male vs. female) between-participants factorial design. Either a male or female experimenter surveyed a male participant who had just crossed either the suspension bridge or a solid bridge. The experimenter then gave out his or her phone number and said that the participant could call him or her if he was interested in the results of the survey. If participants misattributed the cause of their arousal as due to the presence of the female interviewer, participants in the suspension bridge/female interviewer condition would be more likely to call the experimenter. This prediction was confirmed (Figure 5-4). A substantial portion of the male participants in this condition appear to have confused their fear-induced physiological arousal with sexual arousal.

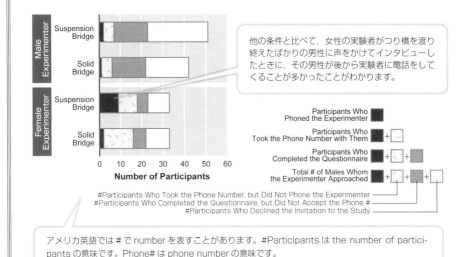

Figure **5**-4. The number of participants as a function of experimenter gender, bridge type, and their responses. [Dutton & Aron, 1974 より筆者作成]

Physiological Arousal：生理的覚醒（または生理的喚起）

Epinephrine：エピネフリン（アドレナリンともいいます）

Thalamus, Hypothalamus：視床，視床下部

Cannon-Bard Theory：キャノン=バード説　　ジェームズ=ランゲ説は脳に感情をつかさどる特定の領域がないと考えています。それに対して，キャノン=バード説は脳の中に感情領域があるという考え方をとっています。

Two-factor Theory of Emotion：情動の二要因理論　　この理論では，生理的覚醒（physiological arousal）と認知的な解釈（情動のラベルづけ）という２つの要因が感情に関わっていると考えます。そのため，原因を誤帰属（misattribution）することで，ラベルが変わってしまう（主観的経験が変わってしまう）と予測されます。

1　Autonomic Nervous System：自律神経系　　自律神経系は内臓との連絡を担う神経で，循環・呼吸・内分泌などと関わっています。ちなみに，Section 5.2 で表情が感情経験に影響することを紹介しましたが，表情は自律神経系によってコントロールされるものではありません。

5.4 Do Emotions Require Cognition?

The two-factor theory of emotion, in addition to its focus on physiological arousal, emphasizes the role of cognition—cognition is necessary because it provides a label for physiological arousal. However, many stimuli are emotionally neutral, and thus do not evoke any arousal. Perhaps cognitive appraisal of stimuli is needed so our brain can determine whether or not to evoke physiological arousal. This is what the proponents of **cognitive appraisal theory** argue (Arnold, 1960; Lazarus, 1966). Accordingly, this theory gives cognition a more important role than the two-factor theory (compare Figures 5-5a and 5-5b).

In support of cognitive appraisal theory, evidence has shown that an externally given "frame" of appraisal moderates people's physiological reaction to an objectively identical stimulus. In one experiment, participants watched a film depicting a subincision (i.e., a penile bisection) ritual in a tribal society under four conditions (Speisman, Lazarus, Mordkoff, & Davison, 1964). In the control condition, participants watched the film without sound. In the *trauma condition*, the film was accompanied by narrations emphasizing pain, cruelty, and danger. In the *intellectualization condition*, the narrator commented on surgical technique. In the *denial condition*, the narrator explained that the ritual would in fact be a happy experience. As expected by cognitive appraisal theory, participants' physiological arousal, measured by skin conductance[1] responses, was highest in the trauma condition, but was much lower in the intellectualization and denial conditions (Figure 5-6). Notice that the two-factor theory cannot explain this finding; it assumes that cognition occurs subsequent to, not before or during, arousal.

Nevertheless, in 1980, Zajonc attacked cognitive appraisal theory by publishing a paper with the subtitle "preferences need no inferences." Zajonc referred to evidence of the subliminal mere exposure effect (see Section 4.3)—even when participants are not consciously aware of target stimuli, they prefer stimuli to which they are repeatedly exposed. In other words, Zajonc argued that some primitive form of emotion (e.g., liking) does not require cognitive processing (i.e., conscious awareness of a stimulus). This led to a debate between a prominent appraisal theorist, Lazarus (1984), and Zajonc (1984). Retrospectively, however, this debate was not over the necessity of initial (cognitive) appraisal, but over definitions of cognition and emotion. To Zajonc, unconscious initial assessment was the beginning of (i.e., part of) emotional reaction; to Lazarus, it was a form of cognition, and was thus something that occurs *prior to* emotional reaction (compare Figures 5-5b and 5-5c). Regardless of which side you take, emotions make use of very quick and crude assessments. For example, you would probably be startled by a snake-like coil of rope on a hiking trail. Your fear response would start well before your brain determined whether it was really dangerous.

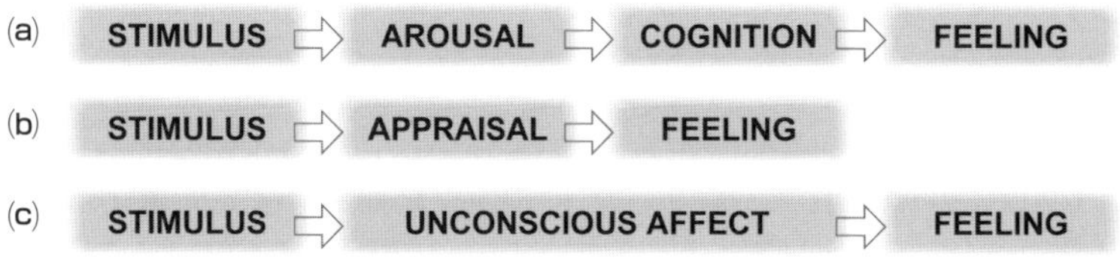

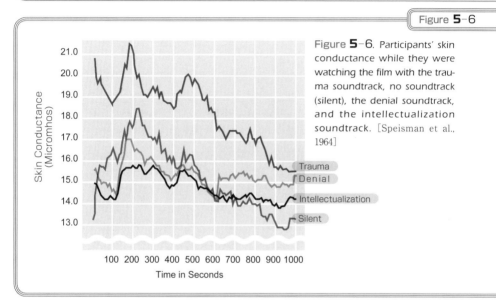

Figure 5-5. Schematic representations of (a) the two-factor theory of emotion, (b) the cognitive appraisal theory, and (c) Zajonc's theory. [LeDoux, 1996, p. 48, p. 52, and 54]

Figure 5-6. Participants' skin conductance while they were watching the film with the trauma soundtrack, no soundtrack (silent), the denial soundtrack, and the intellectualization soundtrack. [Speisman et al., 1964]

Cognitive Appraisal Theory：認知的評価理論　認知的評価理論によれば，ある刺激に対して感情が生起するためには，その刺激の認知的評価が不可欠です。

Figure 5-5a と Figure 5-5b は，LeDoux が著書 *The Emotional Brain* で使用している情動の二要因理論と認知的評価理論の概略図です。これを見比べると，認知的評価理論は認知を感情にとって最初の不可欠な要素と位置づけていることがわかります。

また，Figure 5-5c は Zajonc（1984）の考え方の概略図です。これを Figure 5-5b と見比べると，Zajonc の理論と認知的評価理論（Lazarus の理論）の違いは，主観的経験（フィーリング）を生み出すものを無意識的感情（unconscious affect）と呼ぶか評価（appraisal）と呼ぶかの違いであることがわかります。

1　Skin Conductance：皮膚コンダクタンス　　皮膚の表面の発汗に基づく生理的覚醒の指標です。

5.5 Basic Emotions and Facial Expressions

Can you think of some emotions? If you are Japanese, the common saying consisting of four Chinese characters "喜怒哀楽" might come to mind. Of course, you might notice that certain emotions, such as fear, are absent from this saying. So perhaps you should think of some more. If you search for "emotion" on Wikipedia (in English), you will see a long list of emotions around the top right of your screen—it shows 71 distinct emotions! In psychology textbooks, by contrast, you might see a more modest list containing the six so-called **basic emotions** (i.e., **happiness, sadness, anger, fear, disgust,** and **surprise**). But why are these emotions, and not the other 65, given the privileged moniker of "basic"?

Starting in the 1960s, Ekman and his colleagues embarked upon a decades-long research program to determine which emotions have facial expressions that are universally recognizable. By showing photos of facial expressions and asking participants which emotion matches which face, initial evidence indicated that people in many countries, such as Brazil, Japan, and the U.S.A., readily recognize the facial expressions associated with the six basic emotions (Figure 5-7).

However, Ekman was criticized because all of the abovementioned countries had been exposed to American culture, where the facial expression photographs were originally developed. Therefore, Ekman determined to test his thesis on people who had not previously been exposed to American culture, villagers in a remote area of Papua New Guinea (Ekman & Friesen, 1971). The basic method was to tell a story that typically elicits one of the six basic emotions, and then ask a participant to choose one photograph, from a set of three facial expression photographs, that best fits the story. Examples of the stories are as follows: "His (her) friends have come, and he (she) is happy" for happiness; "His (her) child (mother) has died, and he (she) feels very sad" for sadness (p. 126).

The results are shown in Figure 5-8. Adults in the Papua New Guinea village performed much better than the **chance level** (i.e., 33.3%). Exceptions were when fear and surprise expressions had to be distinguished (the bottom three bars in Figure 5-8. It is noteworthy that this combination (i.e., fear and surprise) was also difficult to distinguish for participants in Ekman and colleagues' earlier studies. Overall, Ekman and Friesen's data from Papua New Guinea can be considered as cogent evidence for the universality of these six facial expressions. If these facial expressions are recognized by people in an isolated village, they plausibly have some biological basis. Therefore, they are called "basic" emotions, which we can expect to encounter all over the world.

Figure 5-7

Happiness　　Sadness　　Anger　　Fear　　Disgust　　Surprise

Figure **5**-7. Facial expressions associated with the six basic emotions.［写真はATR顔表情データベースより（モノクロに改変して掲載）］

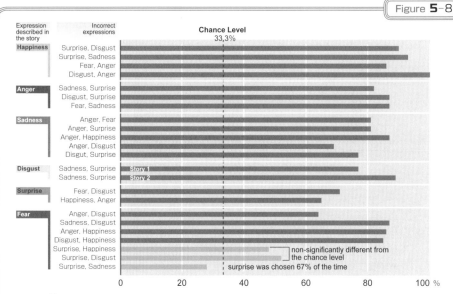

Figure **5**-8. Accurate recognition rate of each facial expression among the Papua New Guinea adult sample.［Ekman & Friesen, 1971より筆者作成］

Basic Emotions：基本情動（基本感情）　　基本情動には**幸福**（**happiness**），悲しみ（**sadness**），怒り（**anger**），恐怖（**fear**），嫌悪（**disgust**），驚き（**surprise**）の6つが含まれます。

📖 **Chance level**　　チャンス・レベルとは，偶然でも正解できる確率です。3つの選択肢があれば，当てずっぽうに答えても3回に1回は正解するはずです。ですから実際の正解率が1/3（＝33.3％）よりも高いかどうかを調べます。Ekman & Friesen（1971）はパプアニューギニアの子どもを対象に選択肢を2つにした実験もしています。子どもたちの正解率もチャンス・レベル（このときには50％）よりも上でした。

References

Arnold, M. B. (1960). *Emotion and personality.* New York: Columbia University Press.

Bower, G. H. (1981). Mood and memory. *American Psychologist, 36,* 129-148. doi: 0.1037/0003-066X.36.2.129

Dutton, G. D., & Aron, A. P. (1974). Some evidence for heightened sexual attraction under conditions of high anxiety. *Journal of Personality and Social Psychology, 30,* 510-517. doi: 10.1037/h0037031

Ekman, P., & Friesen, W. V. (1971). Constants across cultures in the face and emotion. *Journal of Personality and Social Psychology, 17,* 124-129. doi: 10.1037/h0030377

James, W. (1884). What is an emotion? *Mind, 9,* 188-205. doi: 10.1093/mind/os-IX.34.188

Lazarus, R. S. (1966). *Psychological stress and coping process.* New York: McGraw-Hill.

Lazarus, R. S. (1984). On the primacy of cognition. *American Psychologist, 39,* 124-129. doi: 10.1037/0003-066X.39.2.124

LeDoux, J. (1996). *The emotional brain: The mysterious underpinnings of emotional life.* New York: Simon & Schuster. (ルドゥー, J. 松本元ほか (訳) (2003). 『エモーショナル・ブレイン——情動の脳科学』東京大学出版会)

Schachter, S., & Singer, J. (1962). Cognitive, social, and physiological determinants of emotional state. *Psychological Review, 69,* 379-399. doi: 10.1037/h0046234

Speisman, J. C., Lazarus, R. S., Mordkoff, A., & Davison, L. (1964). Experimental reduction of stress based on ego-defense theory. *Journal of Abnormal and Social Psychology, 68,* 367-380. doi: 10.1037/h0048936

Strack, F., Martin, L. L., & Stepper, S. (1988). Inhibiting and facilitating conditions of the human smile: A nonobtrusive test of the facial feedback hypothesis. *Journal of Personality and Social Psychology, 54,* 768-777. doi: 10.1037/0022-3514.54.5.768

Zajonc, R. B. (1980). Feeling and thinking: Preferences need no inferences. *American Psychologist, 35,* 151-175. doi: 10.1037/0003-066X.35.2.151

Zajonc, R. B. (1984). On the primacy of affect. *American Psychologist, 39,* 117-123. doi: 10.1037/0003-066X.39.2.117

CHAPTER 6

Attitudes and Persuasion
態度と説得

6.1
Do Attitudes Predict Behavior?

6.2
What is the Causal Direction of the Attitude-Behavior Relationship?
Cognitive Dissonance Theory

6.3
Persuasion Techniques

6.4
Dual Routes to Persuasion

Advanced Topic
How to Measure Socially Undesirable Attitudes:
The Implicit Association Test

6.1 Do Attitudes Predict Behavior?

The concept of an **attitude** is a somewhat contentious topic in social psychology. On the one hand, one of the founders of the discipline, Gordon Allport[1](1935), was very enthusiastic about attitudes, considering them an indispensable concept. One reason is that attitudes *seemingly* predict behavior. However, at nearly the same time as Allport declared the vital importance of attitudes, a prominent sociologist, LaPiere (1934), published a study that purported to empirically disprove the "attitude-behavior relationship."

During the early 1930s, as racial inequality unsettled the United States, LaPiere traveled across the nation, visiting numerous hotels and restaurants. LaPiere, a white man, was accompanied by a young Chinese married couple, and he let them negotiate arrangements by themselves when possible. Despite prevalent negative attitudes toward the Chinese, the couple were rejected service only once (in total, they stayed at 66 hotels and were served at 188 restaurants and cafes). LaPiere later sent these same establishments a questionnaire with the critical question "Will you accept members of the Chinese race as guests in your establishment?" Of the 47 hotels and 81 restaurants that returned the questionnaire, only one hotel answered YES (43 of the hotels and 73 of the restaurants gave a solid NO, and the rest answered "undecided/depends upon circumstances").

Suspicion about the attitude-behavior relationship culminated when Wicker (1969) published a comprehensive review article showing weak evidence for the attitude-behavior relationship across a wide range of studies. In response to Wicker's criticism, two social psychologists, Fishbein and Ajzen (1974), pointed out a prevalent methodological problem. A single act is determined not only by an attitude but by multiple other factors, yet typical studies employ a single-act criterion. Fishbein and Ajzen maintained that the attitude-behavior relationship should be examined using multiple-act criteria instead.

Weigel and Newman (1976) tested the utility of the multiple-act criteria. They first measured participants' attitudes toward environmental issues. After three months, participants were then asked to sign three environment-related petitions, and to circulate them to their family/friends. Six weeks later, participants were asked to take part in a roadside litter pick-up program. If they agreed, they were then asked to invite their family and friends to participate. Finally, participants were contacted a third time, and were asked to help with a recycling program. They were asked to bundle papers, remove metal parts from bottles, and put these items outside once a week. The experimenter collected the participants' recyclables for eight weeks as a final measure of environmental concern. As shown in Table 6-1, the combined score (an index created from multiple behaviors) is more strongly correlated with participants' environmental attitude (r_{comp}) than is any single behavior (r_{single}).

Table 6-1. Correlation coefficient between participants environmental attitudes and (i) a series of single-act criteria (denoted as r_{single}), (ii) type-wise multiple-act criteria (r_{type}), and (iii) a comprehensive multiple-act criterion (r_{comp}). [Weigel & Newman, 1976]

Single-Act Criteria	r_{single}	Multiple-Act (by Type)	r_{type}	Multiple-Act Criterion	r_{comp}
Sign petition on					
Offshore oil	.41**	Petitioning scale (0-4)	.50**		
Nuclear power	.36**				
Auto exhaust	.39**				
Circulate petitions	.27				
Pick-up litter				Comprehensive behavioral index (i.e., multiple-act criterion)	.62***
As individual	.34*	Litter pick-up scale (0-2)	.36*		
Recruit friend	.22				
Recycling during					
Week 1	.34*	Recycling scale (0-8)	.39**		
Week 2	.57***				
Week 3	.34*				
Week 4	.33*				
Week 5	.12				
Week 6	.20				
Week 7	.20				
Week 8	.34*				

Significance level: * < .05, ** < .01, *** < .001

有意水準を示すアスタリスク　Section 3.1 でも説明したように，心理学の研究結果は統計的に処理されます．このときに，偶然と考えるには起きにくい（5%以下の確率でしか起きない）と判断される場合，その差は統計的に有意である（significant）といいます．有意かどうかは偶然では 1%（または 0.1%）以下の確率でしか起きないという基準でも評価されることがあります．心理学の論文では，上記の表のように * の数で，有意水準（* は 5%，** は 1%，*** は 0.1%）を示すことがあります．

Attitude：態度　　態度は通常，行動と結びつけて考えられがちですが，態度と行動の関係（attitude-behavior relationship）には何度も疑問が投げかけられました．態度が行動と必ずしも結びつかない理由としては，社会的に望ましくない態度は隠される傾向があり，行動としても観察しにくいということもあります．

1　Gordon Allport は 20 世紀前半に活躍した社会心理学者です．彼の兄 Floyd Allport も同時代に活躍した社会心理学者です（Section 7.1 の注 1 を参照）．20 世紀前半の社会心理学の文献を読むときには Allport が 2 人いるので注意して下さい．

CHAPTER **6**　Attitudes and Persuasion

6.2 What is the Causal Direction of the Attitude-Behavior Relationship? Cognitive Dissonance Theory

People typically believe that attitudes cause behavior. Yet as we saw in the previous section, at least when looking at a single act, this often appears to be false. Furthermore, if someone has a socially undesirable attitude (e.g., prejudicial attitude toward a minority group), social norms may well deter that person from behaving in accordance with the attitude—not every prejudicial person spouts hate speech in public. Admitting the absence of a one-to-one correspondence between attitudes and behavior, people still assume that attitudes cause behavior (i.e., "I do it because I like it" / "I don't do it because I don't like it"). However, in the 1950s, under influence of a dominant theory in social psychology, **cognitive dissonance theory** (Festinger, 1957), researchers revealed that the causal order of the attitude-behavior relationship is sometimes the other way around (i.e., "I like it because I did it" / "I don't like it because I didn't do it").

According to cognitive dissonance theory, people prefer to think and act in ways that are consistent. Thus, when our thoughts fail to match our actions, or vice versa, we experience psychological discomfort. We then seek to reduce this discomfort by changing either our attitude or behavior. For example, many of us love to eat *sushi* such as fatty tuna. But how do we feel when we consider that bluefin tuna is an endangered species? Obviously it is difficult to both enjoy eating Bluefin Tuna at the same time we know we are contributing to its extinction. Being acquainted with this information, someone might stop eating tuna. So as Festinger explained, this person might change his or her attitude in accordance with his or her behavior (e.g., "I don't like tuna anyway"). But is this just an instance of *sour grapes*?

Aronson and Carlsmith (1963) experimentally tested cognitive dissonance theory with young children (around 5 years old). They showed a set of five toys to each child, and determined his or her preference for each toy. Next, the experimenter selected the child's second-preferred toy and forbid him or her from playing with it during the experimenter's brief absence from the room. In the mild threat condition, the experimenter explained that if the child played with the toy, the experimenter "would be annoyed," whereas in the severe threat condition, the experimenter "would be very angry," and would take away all five toys. In both conditions, children did not play with the forbidden toy while the experimenter left the room. After the experimenter returned, children were allowed to play with the five toys, and were asked their preferences again. Consistent with cognitive dissonance theory, only children in the mild threat condition decreased their liking for the forbidden toy. Why? Because not playing with the toy, despite being able to, caused dissonance. In order to reduce the dissonance, children updated their attitude to reflect their past behavior. In this way, a behavior (not playing) caused an attitude (not liking)!

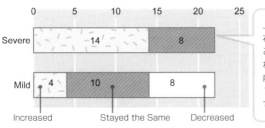

Figure **6**-1. The number of children whose preference for the second-preferred toy increased, stayed the same, or decreased as a function of the threat condition. [Aronson & Carlsmith, 1963 より筆者作成]

Cognitive Dissonance Theory：認知的不協和理論　認知的不協和理論によれば，自分の信念や態度と行動が一貫しないと不快感（認知的不協和）が生じます。私たちはこの不快感を軽減しようとすると予測されます。このとき，すでに済んでしまった行動の場合は行動を変更することができないので態度や信念が変化すると予測されます。

　Aronson & Carlsmith（1963）の実験では，玩具が好きだという態度とそれで遊ばないという行動が不協和を生じさせます。このときに，きつい禁止があれば遊ばないことは簡単に正当化できるので，態度を変化させる必要がありません（「本当は遊びたいけれど，遊んだら怒られるから遊ばないのだ」と考えることができます）。一方，禁止がそれほど強くないとそれによって正当化できないので，「遊ばないのは，本当はそれほど好きではないからだ」と態度を変化させる必要があるというわけです。

　これはイソップ童話の「すっぱいブドウ」を連想させます。高いところになったおいしそうなブドウを食べることができなかったキツネは「どうせすっぱいのさ」と負け惜しみをいいました。認知的不協和理論によれば，ただの負け惜しみではなく，本当に態度が変わるのです。

　ちなみに，この童話から，英語で sour grapes には「負け惜しみ」という意味があります。

CHAPTER **6**　Attitudes and Persuasion

6.3 Persuasion Techniques

Have you ever been asked to do a small favor for a salesperson, for example, to fill out a brief questionnaire about a company's products? If you complied with the salesperson's request, did it influence your subsequent behavior? You might think it didn't. However, social psychological evidence suggests it did. People are more likely to comply with a large request (e.g., to buy a salesperson's product) if they have already complied with a small request. This is called the **foot-in-the-door technique**, after the conventional sales tactic of asking someone to open their door and just listen for a few minutes.

In a classic experiment, researchers called a group of housewives first to ask a small favor (i.e., to answer a brief survey about household products), and later to ask a substantially larger favor (i.e., to allow five or six men to conduct an intensive survey at their home three days later) (Freedman & Fraser, 1966). Researchers were interested in whether the initial small request would increase the number of participants who would comply with the second larger request. They included three additional conditions. In the agree-only condition, once a housewife agreed to take the survey, the experimenter hung up the phone saying he had another call. In the familiarization condition, the experimenter simply introduced the name of the supposed survey company. Finally, in the one-contact condition, participants received only the second call. The results support the effectiveness of the foot-in-the-door technique. As shown in Figure 6-2, the percentage of participants who complied with the second request was highest when this technique was used. (By the way, the denominator of this percentage includes both those people who accepted and refused the first request, that is, both people who are inherently more or less compliant.)

Nevertheless, please do not rush to the conclusion that asking a small favor is always the best tactic. In some cases, an initial large request increases subsequent compliance. This is called the **door-in-the-face technique**. Your initial large request is likely to be refused (as if a door has been closed in your face), such that your target may feel somewhat guilty. If you next ask a small request, your target may accept this as a concession, and feel obliged to make a concession for you. As a result, your target is more likely to comply with your small, real request, following a large decoy request.

In one experiment (Cialdini et al., 1975), participants were asked to engage in a volunteer activity—taking juvenile delinquents on a two-hour trip to a local zoo. One third of participants were first asked to engage in a much larger volunteer activity—serving as a counselor for juvenile delinquents for a minimum period of two-years. Compared to those who were only given the small request, and those who were given these two requests simultaneously, those who were initially given (but refused) the large request were substantially more likely to comply with the request to take the trip to the zoo (See Figure 6-3).

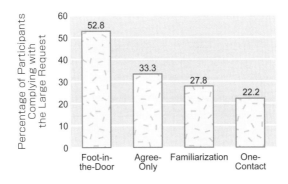

Figure 6-2. The percentage of participants who complied with the large request (an intensive survey) in each experimental condition. [Freedman & Fraser, 1966 より筆者作成]

Foot-in-the-Door Technique：フット・イン・ザ・ドア・テクニック　最初に小さなお願いを了承してもらい，少しずつ要求をつりあげていく説得方法のことです。

Door-in-the-Face Technique：ドア・イン・ザ・フェース・テクニック　最初に相手が絶対に了承しないような大きなお願いをして断らせた後，自分も譲歩するからそちらも譲歩してほしいというかたちで本来の依頼を了承させる説得方法のことです。

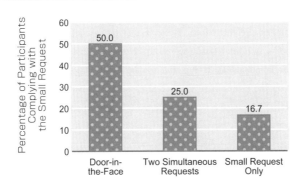

Figure 6-3. The percentage of participants who complied with the small request (a two-hour trip to a zoo) in each experimental condition. [Cialdini et al., 1975 より筆者作成]

CHAPTER 6　Attitudes and Persuasion

6.4 Dual Routes to Persuasion

Advertisements for health-care programs often tout medical doctors' approval without any scientific evidence. Perhaps this is because marketers know that even weak arguments are likely to be accepted when they come from a credible source (Aronson, Turner, & Carlsmith, 1963). Indeed, source credibility can be a useful tool for deciding whether or not to accept a persuasive argument.

In reality, however, it is best to focus more on the central component of an argument (i.e., argument quality), rather than peripheral cues (e.g., source credibility). According to the **dual process model of persuasion**, which part of an argument you will tend to consider depends on how much you are involved with the issue. This was tested by Petty, Cacioppo, and Goldman (1981). In their classic study, they tried to persuade a group of university students to accept the following, rather difficult to accept, proposition: All students must pass a final exam in order to graduate.

This study employed a complex design. First, to manipulate *argument quality*, some students were presented with convincing statistical analyses that linked final exams and improvements in education, while some students were presented with mere **anecdotes**. Second, to manipulate *source credibility*, some students were told the argument was from a source high in expertise (i.e., a professor of education at Princeton University), and some were told it was from a source low in expertise (i.e., a group of local high school students). Finally, to manipulate *personal involvement*, the researchers told half the students that the exam would be instituted next year—they would have to take the exam themselves, and half the students that the exam would be instituted in 10 years.

As expected, students were more persuaded when the source was high in expertise, as well as when they received high, as opposed to low, quality arguments in support of the proposition. However, the most interesting results of this study have to do with personal involvement, that is, whether students thought they themselves would have to take the exam next year (or someone else would have to take it). Highly involved students were much more influenced by the strength of the arguments—the central route to persuasion. (In the left panel of Figure 6-4, see the large difference that corresponds with high vs. low argument quality.) On the other hand, when students thought they wouldn't have to take the exam, superficial cues of source credibility—the peripheral route to persuasion—were more important. (See the low involvement panel; the expert-nonexpert difference is more informative of whether students preferred the exam than the difference based on argument quality.) This study makes it clear that there are two different, at times even contradictory, routes (or dual processes) to persuasion.

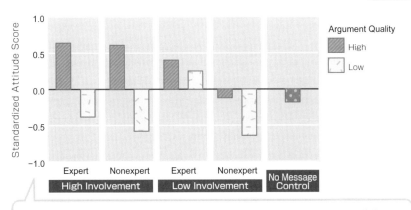

Figure **6**-4. Standardized attitude scores (preference for the new test) as a function of argument quality, source credibility, and involvement along with the attitude score in the no message control condition.［Petty et al., 1981 より筆者作成］

Dual Process Model of Persuasion：説得の二重過程モデル　　説得メッセージに関わる情報処理には2種類あるという考え方です。2種類というのは，「メッセージの内容それ自体の説得力に着目する情報処理」と「情報源の信頼性など周辺的な情報に着目する情報処理」のことです。

　二重過程モデルのひとつ，精緻化見込みモデル（elaboration likelihood model）では，前者を中心ルート（central route），後者を周辺ルート（peripheral route）の情報処理といいます。もうひとつの二重過程モデルであるヒューリスティック・システマティックモデル（heuristic-systematic model）では前者をシステマティック処理，後者をヒューリスティック処理といいます。

📖 **Anecdote**　　Anecdote とは辞書的には逸話という意味です。これは，科学的な証拠のような体系だった証拠に対して，いくつかの事例だけに基づいた証拠のような意味で用いられることがあります。この場合，anecdotal evidence という表現もよく用いられます。

Advanced Topic

How to Measure Socially Undesirable Attitudes:
The Implicit Association Test

So far, we have presented studies that use **self-report** measures of attitudes. In other words, participants are asked to explicitly rate their attitudes by themselves using a certain scale (e.g., from 1 = "strongly disagree" to 7 = "strongly agree"). However, if we ask about socially undesirable attitudes, such as racism, do participants honestly report their attitudes? Reputational concerns might distort responses—after all, it is extremely easy for racists to disguise their racism by dishonestly checking "1" (i.e., indicating a strong disagreement with the idea of racism) instead of "7." There is a measure called the **implicit association test (IAT)** that can substantially reduce attitudinal concealment due to reputational concern (Greenwald, McGhee, & Schwartz, 1998). The IAT makes use of response latency, which is beyond conscious control.

In Greenwald et al.'s experiment, white American participants undertook a series of computerized categorization tasks that involved choosing—as quickly as possible—whether a word (presented in the center of the screen) belonged to a category displayed in the upper left- or upper right-hand corner of the screen. First, participants categorized typical *black* names (e.g., Ebony, Tia) versus typical *white* names (e.g., Nancy, Peggy)[1]. Second, they categorized pleasant words (e.g., lucky, honor) versus unpleasant words (e.g., evil, ugly). In the third task, the first two practice tasks were combined. Participants had to respond to *black* names and pleasant words with one key, while responding to *white* names and unpleasant words with another key. This third task is supposed to be difficult for people possessing racial prejudice—in their belief system, black people tend to be associated with unpleasant traits. As shown in Figure 6–5, response latency was substantially longer during the third task, which reflects some sort of difficulty in performing this task.

Although the above pattern suggests the presence of implicit (anti-black) racial bias, perhaps the slower responses during the third task had to do with its greater complexity because it combines two tasks. To eliminate this possibility, Greenwald et al. included two further tasks. The fourth task was a mirror-image version of the first task; participants still had to categorize *black* versus *white* names, but the categories now appeared in the opposite corners of the screen (i.e., *white* versus *black*). The fifth task involved categorizing *white* + pleasant versus *black* + unpleasant (i.e., the fourth task combined with the second task). Notice that this categorization pattern is congruent with anti-black prejudice. Response latency for the fifth task was shorter than the third task, and almost equivalent to that of tasks one, two, and four! In a sense, task five was "easy." The difference in latency between the third task (*black* + pleasant / *white* + unpleasant) and the fifth task (*white* + pleasant / *black* + unpleasant) is called the IAT effect, and it is considered to indicate the strength of implicit racial attitudes.

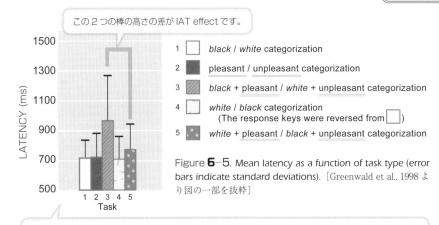

Figure **6**-5. Mean latency as a function of task type (error bars indicate standard deviations). [Greenwald et al., 1998 より図の一部を抜粋]

この図は本文で説明している IAT 実験の進行に対応しています。まず *black*（黒人）と *white*（白人）のいずれかに典型的な名前が提示されたときに左右のキーで反応する練習，次に pleasant（快）または unpleasant（不快）な単語のいずれかが提示されたときに左右のキーで反応する練習をします。その後，*black* と pleasant のいずれかが提示されたときには左キーで反応し，*white* と unpleasant のいずれかが提示されたときには右キーで反応する課題を行います。次に最初の練習を逆転させた *white* と *black* に左右のキーで反応する練習をして，*white* と pleasant のいずれかが提示されたときに左キーで反応し，*black* と unpleasant のいずれかが提示されたときに右キーで反応する課題を行います。このうち 3 番目と 5 番目に行う人種と快・不快への反応を組み合わせた課題が IAT 効果を計算するために必要な課題です。Greenwald らの実験では，この 2 つの課題を逆の順序で行う条件を（参加者内・参加者間要因配置の両方のやり方で）設けることで，IAT 効果が課題を行う順序によって観察されたり観察されなくなったりするという可能性を排除しています。

Implicit Association Test（IAT）：潜在連合テスト 潜在連合テストは，**自己報告（self-report）**式の態度測定では社会的に望ましくない態度を意識的に隠すことができるという問題を回避するための態度測定方法です。

IAT で測定される態度は潜在態度（implicit attitude），自己報告式による態度は顕在態度（explicit attitude）といいます。潜在態度は単に意識的に隠蔽されるものではなく，本人も自覚していない態度だと考える研究者もいます。この場合は，顕在態度と潜在態度はそれぞれ自覚される態度と自覚されない態度を測定していると考えます（IAT を用いた研究の例として，CHAPTER 8 の Advanced Topic も参照してください）。

ただし，IAT を差別的態度の測定に利用することには批判もあります。IAT への批判のまとめとしては，以下のアメリカ心理学会のサイトに掲載されている記事が参考になります。

http://www.apa.org/monitor/2008/07-08/psychometric.aspx

---

1 IAT の説明にあたって，IAT で態度を測定しようとする対象（黒人と白人）を斜体で示しています。IAT では，これを明らかに好ましい・好ましくない対象と組み合わせます。ここでは pleasant（快）な単語と unpleasant（不快）な単語がそれにあたります。これらには二重線を引いて示しています。

References

Allport, G. W. (1935). Attitudes. In C. Murchison (Ed.), *Handbook of social psychology* (pp. 798-844). Worcester, MA: Clark University Press.

Aronson, E., & Carlsmith, J. M. (1963). Effect of the severity of threat on the devaluation of forbidden behavior. *Journal of Abnormal and Social Psychology, 66*, 584-588. doi: 10.1037/h0039901

Aronson, E., Turner, J., & Carlsmith, J. M. (1963). Communicator credibility and communication discrepancy as determinants of opinion change. *Journal of Abnormal and Social Psychology, 67*, 31-36. doi: 10.1037/h0045513

Cialdini, R. B., Vincent, J. E., Lewis, S. K., Catalan, J., Wheeler, D., & Darby, B. L. (1975). Reciprocal concessions procedure for inducing compliance: The door-in-the-face technique. *Journal of Personality and Social Psychology, 31*, 206-215. doi: 10.1037/h0076284

Festinger, L. (1957). *A theory of cognitive dissonance.* Stanford, CA: Stanford University Press.

Fishbein, M., & Ajzen, I. (1974). Attitudes towards objects as predictors of single and multiple behavioral criteria. *Psychological Review, 81*, 59-74. doi: http://dx.doi.org/10.1037/h0035872

Freedman, J. L., & Fraser, S. C. (1966). Compliance without pressure: The foot-in-the-door technique. *Journal of Personality and Social Psychology, 4*, 195-202. doi: 10.1037/h0023552

Greenwald, A. G., McGhee, D. E., & Schwartz, J. L. K. (1998). Measuring individual differences in implicit cognition: The implicit association test. *Journal of Personality and Social Psychology, 74*, 1464-1480. doi: 10.1037/0022-3514.74.6.1464

LaPiere, R. T. (1934). Attitudes vs. actions. *Social Forces, 13*, 230-237. doi: 10.2307/2570339

Petty, R. E., Cacioppo, J. T., & Goldman, R. (1981). Personal involvement as a determinant of argument-based persuasion. *Journal of Personality and Social Psychology, 41*, 847-855. doi: 10.1037/0022-3514.41.5.847

Weigel, R. H., & Newman, L. S. (1976). Increasing attitude-behavior correspondence by broadening the scope of the behavioral measure. *Journal of Personality and Social Psychology, 33*, 793-802. doi: 10.1037/0022-3514.33.6.793

Wicker, A. W. (1969). Attitudes versus actions: The relationship of verbal and overt behavioral responses to attitude objects. *Journal of Social Issues, 25*, 41-78. doi: 10.1111/j.1540-4560.1969.tb00619.x

CHAPTER 7

Social Influence
社会的影響

7.1
The Influence of Social Settings: Social Facilitation

7.2
Social Loafing

7.3
Conformity to the Majority Ⅰ

7.4
Conformity to the Majority Ⅱ

7.5
Minority Influence

Advanced Topic
Social Exclusion Hurts

7.1 The Influence of Social Settings: Social Facilitation

Imagine you have been diligently practicing a challenging piece of music (e.g., the 3rd movement of Beethoven's Moonlight Sonata) on the piano. Now that you have mastered it, it's time to perform in front of an audience. Will you play better or worse than usual? In other words, how will the presence of other people (a social setting) influence your performance? This is one of the oldest questions experimentally tackled by social psychologists.

More than a century ago, an American psychologist, Triplett, noticed that bicycle racers were faster when they competed against other racers than when they pedaled alone. He suspected that when many people simultaneously engage in the same task, in a **"co-action** setting," each individual performs better than when engaging in the same task alone. In order to test this idea, he conducted what is presumably the first published social psychological experiment; it involved children, either in pairs or alone, reeling in a certain length of fishing line as fast as possible (Triplett, 1898). Triplett found that there was a tendency for children to reel faster when they were performing the task alongside other children. This finding, that the presence of co-actors enhances performance, is now subsumed under the rubric of **social facilitation**, which occurs due to the presence of either an **audience** or co-actor(s).

Approximately two decades later, Floyd Allport[1] (1920) published the results of a series of experiments that deepened our understanding of how audiences affect not only behavior but also cognition. He had participants engage in the so-called chain association task (i.e., writing a chain of words, each of which must be conceptually associated with the previous word) either alone or in a group. Participants wrote more words within three minutes in the group condition than in the alone condition. In the article, however, Allport noted one exception. When participants engaged in a complex cognitive task (i.e., producing multiple, strong counterarguments to philosophical claims), the presence of co-actors impaired the quality of arguments (but still increased the sheer number of arguments).

It was not until 1965 that someone provided a theoretical integration of these phenomena. Combining findings from animal research (e.g., rats eat more in the presence of conspecifics than when alone) and human research, such as Allport's, Zajonc proposed the theory of social facilitation: the presence of others, regardless of whether they are co-actors or an audience, induces arousal, which in turn facilitates performance on well-learned tasks, but undermines performance on complex or unlearned tasks.

Returning to the piano example, the key component that determines whether you will deliver an excellent performance is practice. In this chapter, we will learn more about how people are influenced, changed, by the presence of others.

Social Facilitation：社会的促進　　他者と一緒に作業をすること，または誰かに見られることで課題遂行成績が上昇することを社会的促進といいます。

同じ作業を一緒にすることは **co-action**（定訳はありませんが，あえて訳すなら**共行為**）状況と呼ばれます。共行為状況と観察者（**audience**）がいる状況（あなたが作業をしているところを誰かに見られている状況）では，社会的促進が生じることが知られています。

ただし，この社会的促進効果は単純な課題を行う場合に限られており，複雑な課題を行う状況ではむしろ社会的抑制（social inhibition）が生じます。

> 補足4　社会的促進は教科書にもよく取りあげられる現象ですが，実はその効果はさほど大きくないかもしれません。例えば Triplett のデータを見ると，確かに自転車レースの選手は単独で記録を作ろうとするときよりもペースメーカーがついているときに記録がよく，ペースメーカーがいるときよりも他の選手と競争しているときに，さらに記録がよくなっていました（1マイルを単独のときに2分29.9秒，ペースメーカーがいるときに1分55.5秒，他の選手との競争のときに1分50.35秒かかっていました）。しかし，この効果はペースメーカーによってペース配分がうまくいくことや，ライバルとの競争心などさまざまな要因で説明できそうです。子どものリール巻きの結果もさほどはっきりしたものではありませんでした。社会的促進を示した子どもは確かに10人いたのですが，効果がなかった子どもが5人，促進ではなく抑制を示した子どもも5人いました。また，Allport の実験結果も，おしなべて強い効果ではありませんでした。
>
> 過去の研究結果を集めてまとめて分析しなおす手法をメタ分析（meta-analysis）といいますが，社会的促進研究についても241の実験を集めたメタ分析が行われています（Bond & Titus, 1983）。その結果，さまざまな実験課題をぜんぶまとめてしまうと社会的促進効果は非常に弱く，単純な作業のスピードを少し上げる効果が見られる程度だということです。単純な作業でも正確さは上昇しないと著者らは述べています。また，複雑な作業の場合，確かに抑制が見られるのですが，その効果も成績のバラつきの1%から3%程度の小さなものだったということです。

1　Section 6.1 の注でも述べたように，20世紀前半には2人の Allport という名前の著名な社会心理学者が活躍していました。Floyd Allport は Section 6.1 で登場した Gordon Allport の兄です。

7.2 Social Loafing

In many situations, you are not just co-acting with other people, you are cooperating. Consider the simple example of tug-of-war.[1] Winning tug-of-war hinges not only on your own effort but also, critically, on your teammates' efforts. Unlike social facilitation, in this setting, each member may feel they don't have to perform at their best because the team will pick up the slack. Thus a **diffusion of responsibility** may occur, which reduces each member's motivation to perform—a **motivation loss**. In other words, people may become motivated to **free-ride** (or **free-load**) on the efforts of others, resulting in the phenomenon of **social loafing**.

Nevertheless, even when each member performs at their best, group performance can still fall short. This is due to a flaw in coordination—a **coordination loss** (Steiner, 1972). For example, in tug-of-war, if each member pulls the rope in slightly different directions at their own pace, this causes a reduction in coordination. Therefore, to maximize group performance, the group must pull the rope in the same direction at a synchronized pace.

There is an elegant experiment that illustrates the importance of both motivation loss (i.e., social loafing) and coordination loss. Latané and colleagues asked participants to shout as loudly as possible either alone, in a pair, or in a six-person group (Latané, Williams, & Harkins, 1979). The pairs' performance fell short of the sum of two alone performances. Similarly, the six-person groups' performance did not even amount to half of the sum of six alone performances. Notice that these reductions can be due to either social loafing, coordination loss, or both.

To determine what proportion of the reduced performance was attributable to social loafing, the researchers led some participants to believe that they were shouting with one other participant or five other participants, even though they were actually shouting by themselves (while wearing a blindfold and sound-proof headphones). These were called the pseudo group conditions. As shown in Figure 7-1, participants shouted less loudly when they believed they were shouting in groups (the pseudo group condition) than when alone (the 1.0 baseline). This effect is designated by the light gray area in Figure 7-1.

Nonetheless, the actual groups' performance declined even more sharply than the pseudo groups' performance. Social loafing alone is not sufficient to account for the reduced performance of actual groups. Coordination loss explains the extra reduction in performance (the dark gray area in Figure 7-1). Although these real groups attempted to maximize the loudness of their shouting, it was difficult for everyone to shout at the maximum level at exactly the same time. This difficulty with coordination explains why each member's loudness (i.e., the actual group's loudness divided by the number of group members) was lower than that of the pseudo group.

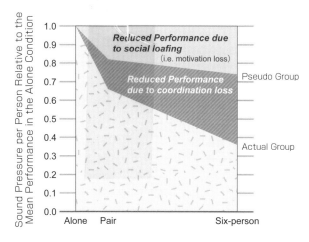

Figure **7**-1. Sound pressure per person as a function of group size and group type (pseudo vs. actual). [Latané et al., 1979]

Social Loafing：社会的手抜き　集団での作業で，評価が集団単位でなされる場合に，作業への動機づけが低下することがあります。これを社会的手抜きといいます。他の人がやるから自分が全力を出さなくても大丈夫というふうに**責任の分散**（**diffusion of responsibility**）が生じ，他人の努力に**ただ乗り**（**free-ride/free-load**）しようとするためです（責任の分散は Section 9.4，ただ乗りの問題は CHAPTER 9 の Advanced Topic でも出てきます）。

Coordination Loss：調整の失敗　Steiner（1972）は集団の成績が個人の成績の単純な和を下回る理由として，各人の動機づけが低下する**動機づけの低下**（**motivation loss**）だけでなく「調整の失敗」があることを指摘しました。

1　集団で綱引き（tug-of-war）をするときの力が個々人の力の総和より小さくなってしまうことは，20世紀初頭に発見されました。発見者の名前から，これをリンゲルマン効果（Ringelmann effect）ともいいます。

7.3 Conformity to the Majority I

Imagine that you are in a group of eight people taking part in a psychology experiment. The experimenter shows you three lines of differing length, along with a target line. The experimenter asks each of the eight participants which of the three test lines (1, 2, or 3) is the same length as the target line. You are the seventh participant, and everyone before you chose the correct line. You also choose the correct one. The experimenter continues this procedure with a different set of lines, and everyone gets the correct answer again. This is a pretty boring experiment, isn't it? However, something weird happens during the third round. The experimenter shows a new set of target and test lines (see Figure 7-2). Again, you think the answer is obvious. The answer is 1, right? However, the first participant chooses the second line. You might think to yourself, "How can that person get this easy question wrong?" But the second participant also chooses the second line. Subsequent participants do so, too. Now it's your turn. Which line do you choose? Do you choose the one that you think is correct, line 1? Or do you go along with the crowd?

This is the actual experiment that was conducted by Asch to investigate **conformity** (Asch, 1951, 1955). In the above example, other apparent participants, in fact experimental **confederates**, made errors on predetermined rounds (specifically, they made errors during 12 out of 18 total rounds). Did Asch's participants, mid-20th century American university students, conform to the confederates, or did they overcome the social pressure? Despite the American education system, which emphasizes the importance of autonomy and uniqueness, 74% of participants conformed to the wrong majority at least once during the experiment. However, there were large individual differences among these conformists: some conformed just once during the 12 critical rounds, while some conformed during 11 of the 12 rounds. On average, participants conformed during 32% of these critical rounds.

Asch included several variations in his experiment. For example, he tested the effect of a "fellow dissenter"—What if there is someone who goes against the majority? When there was a dissenting confederate who consistently chose the correct line, the conformity rate dropped precipitously to 5.6%. The importance of a fellow dissenter was also illustrated in another variation of the experiment, where the fellow dissenter started to conform to the majority around the middle of the experiment. This caused an abrupt rise in the conformity rate to 28.5%, which is almost the same as the original conformity rate. On the other hand, if one of the incorrect majority started to choose the correct line during the middle of the experiment, this caused the conformity rate to drop down to 7.8%. As we can see from Asch's classic research on conformity, the **unanimity** of a group makes it very hard to voice the proverbial objection, "But he isn't wearing anything at all!"[1]

 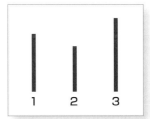

Figure **7**-2. The sample stimuli of Asch's experiment. The left panel shows the target, and the right panel shows the three options.

Conformity：同調　　他の人たちの意見によって自分の意見や行動を変えることを同調といいます。次の Section 7.4 で詳しく見ますが，意見はそのままで行動だけみんなと合わせることもあるでしょうし，意見までみんなに合わせて変えてしまうこともあるでしょう。

Confederate：(実験の) **サクラ**　　社会心理学の実験では，参加者にわからないように実験協力者に演技をしてもらったりして，参加者に実際とは違う状況にいると信じてもらうことがあります。このときの実験協力者をサクラといいます。英語では confederate 以外にも stooge という用語が使われていることがあります。

📖 **Unanimity**：全員一致（形容詞は unanimous）　　この言葉は，話し合いのルールのひとつとして出てくることがあります。一般的なのは多数決ルール（majority rule）でしょう。それに対して全員が賛成しないと決めることができないというルールは全員一致ルール（unanimity rule）といわれます。

1　But he isn't wearing anything at all!　　『裸の王様』（英語のタイトルは *The Emperor's New Clothes*）の最後で，小さな子どもが叫ぶ言葉です。日本語では「王様は裸だ！」となっています。

7.4 Conformity to the Majority II

Researchers have investigated both quantitative and qualitative aspects of majority influence. Asch investigated the quantitative side of majority influence by systematically varying the number of confederates. As shown in Figure 7-3, participants did not choose the wrong lines when they were alone (i.e., when the number of confederates was zero). One confederate also did not cause much conformity. However, the presence of two consensually wrong confederates increased the frequency that participants would choose the wrong lines—the mean number of errors was 1.5, which was still low given that the maximum number of errors was 12. Once the number of confederates hit three, however, conformity reached its maximum rate—additional confederates did not increase conformity rates.

The quantitative aspect of **social influence** was formalized by Latané (1981) as the **social impact theory**. According to this theory, the impact of a source is a function of its *strength*, *immediacy*, and *number*. We are more likely to conform to stronger sources (e.g., more salient, powerful, and/or important sources). We are more likely to conform to more immediate sources than distant sources. And we are more likely to conform to sources greater in number. This formalization fits the results of many conformity studies.

The qualitative aspect of conformity is captured by the dichotomy of **informational influence** and **normative influence** (Deutsch & Gerard, 1955). Some participants in Asch's experiment were subject to informational influence—they genuinely thought the other participants were right, and they were wrong (e.g., maybe it looks different from my angle). In other words, these participants considered the confederates to be a credible source of information, and went with them due to a *desire to be right*. Other participants were subject to normative influence—they tried to get along with others (e.g., maybe other people will dislike me if I behave in a deviant manner). These participants conformed to the majority due to a *desire to be liked*.

To separate these two types of social influence, Deutsch and Gerard conducted a complicated experiment. Here we present only a part of their experiment (and thus present it as a 2 × 2 factorial design). They ran an Asch-like experiment in an anonymous setting. Some participants were told that the group as a whole would be rewarded (receive Broadway tickets) based on the group's performance. Others were not told about this reward. This condition was crossed with the availability of the target line, making the correct choice either more or less obvious. The results are shown in Figure 7-4. The effect of group reward (i.e., the left vs. right side of the figure) reflects normative influence (participants didn't want to bother others when a desirable reward was at stake). The effect of target availability (i.e., the different patterned bars) reflects informational influence. Increasing uncertainty causes participants to rely on others' judgments.

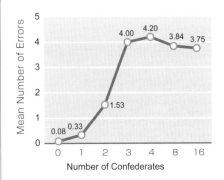

Figure 7-3. The mean number of errors in Asch's experiment as a function of the number of confederates. [Asch, 1951 より筆者作成]

Figure 7-4. The mean number of socially influenced errors as a function of the presence of reward (normative pressure) and the availability of the targets (informational uncertainty). [Deutsch & Gerard, 1955 より筆者作成]

Two Types of **Social Influence**：(2種類の) **社会的影響**　本章のタイトルは広い意味での社会的な影響です。ですが，社会心理学では，社会的影響を同調の要因という狭い意味で使うこともあります。この場合，社会的影響は**情報的影響**（**informational influence**）と**規範的影響**（**normative influence**）の大きく2つに分けられます。

　他者の意見が正しいと思い，自分も正しい判断がしたいと考えて他者に同調するなら情報的影響を受けていることになります。

　反対意見を言うとみんなから嫌がられるのではないかと考えて同調するときには，規範的影響を受けていることになります。

Social Impact Theory：**社会的インパクト理論**　Latané（1981）は，社会的影響力の大きさは影響源の強さ（strength）・近さ（immediacy）・数（number）の関数で決まると考えました。

7.5 Minority Influence

Have you ever watched the classic film, *Twelve Angry Men*[1]? The film depicts the total opposite of Asch's experiment. The twelve men are jurors[2] who are appointed to make a guilty vs. not guilty judgment in a murder case. Nearly every juror considers the defendant, a juvenile delinquent, to be guilty. However, one juror considers that the evidence presented in the court is not beyond a reasonable doubt, and thus that it is a mistake to conclude the defendant is guilty. Little-by-little, the dissenting juror demonstrates how each piece of evidence is invalid or imperfect, and one-by-one the other jurors convert their judgment from guilty to not guilty. Finally, all twelve jurors unanimously reach their verdict—not guilty. It is an amazing (and highly recommended) film, but a natural question for you, having just studied Asch's experiment, is as follows: Can a single person really change the mind of a majority?

Moscovici and colleagues tried to answer this question using a social psychological experiment (Moscovici, Lage, & Naffrechoux, 1969). Although they were familiar with Asch's findings, they thought that in at least some circumstances a small minority could successfully introduce new ideas to a majority. Thus, they conducted a reverse version of Asch's experiment: Two confederates played the role of the minority in six-person groups that were tasked with naming the color of a series of 36 (all blue) slides.

In one of the experimental conditions, two confederates consistently said "the slide is green" throughout the 36 trials. In the other experimental condition, the confederates said "the slide is green" in just 24 of the 36 trials, and thus their responses were inconsistent. Finally, in the control condition, the groups consisted of only **naive participants**. As shown in Figure 7-5, the consistent minority succeeded in inducing some "green" responses from the real participants. You might be tempted to note that this only occured in 8.42% of the trials. But remember that the conformity rate to the unanimous majority was only 33% in Asch's experiment. More importantly, in the control and inconsistent minority conditions, virtually no participants said "the slide is green." Therefore, this experiment clearly demonstrates that it is possible for *consistent* minority members to exert their influence.

Some researchers consider that minority influence is qualitatively different from majority influence. Nemeth (1986), for example, argues that the minority's view point, if accepted, broadens thoughts about the focal issue. In other words, targets of minority influence start to think about the issue in some novel ways. If you find yourself in a minority position, but are sure that you are right, be brave to express your opinion in a confident and consistent manner—at the least you can make others think, and at the most, you may even make them change their minds!

Figure **7**-5

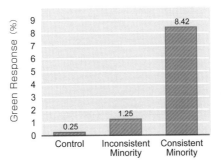

Figure **7**-5. The percent of the minority confederates who succeeded to exert minority influence as a function of consistency. [Moscovici et al., 1969 より筆者作成]

> 補足5　左ページを読んで,「陪審裁判でたった1人の少数派の陪審員が影響力をもつことが本当にあるのか？」という疑問をもったかもしれません。この質問に対する答えは「ほとんどない」というものです。現実の陪審の評決を事例分析した古典的な陪審裁判研究では, 少数派の陪審員の意見が最終的な評決となったのは10回に1回程度と報告されています (Kalven & Zeisel, 1966)。ただし, ここでの少数派には12人中4, 5人程度の少数派も含まれていることに注意してください。実際の陪審裁判での少数派は, 12人中たった1人という少数派よりも, このような半数をやや下回る程度の少数派がほとんどだったはずです。このように考えると, 12人中1人だけの少数派の意見が最終的な評決となるのは極めて稀なことだといえるでしょう。しかし, これは陪審裁判がうまく機能していないことを意味するわけではありません。裁判で提示される証拠を吟味した上で, 12人のうち11人が解釈を誤るというような状況が生じる確率がとても小さいということなのです。

Naive participants　Naiveを辞書で調べると「世間知らずな」「だまされやすい」といった訳語があてられています。しかし, 実験の参加者がnaiveだというときには「実験の仮説を知らず, 過去に同様の実験に参加したことのない」という意味になります。左ページでは「仮説を知らない（サクラではない）参加者いう意味で使っています。

また, naiveはもともとフランス語の単語で, 英語の文章の中でもフランス語のスペルをそのまま使ってnaïveと書かれていることがしばしばあります。

1　Twelve Angry Men：邦題『12人の怒れる男』　陪審裁判を描いた有名な映画です。
2　Jury：陪審　アメリカの裁判は, 一般市民から選ばれた12人の陪審員 (juror) からなる陪審 (jury) によって有罪 (guilty)・有罪ではない (not guilty) の評決 (verdict) が下されます（ただし, 陪審は量刑の判断はしません）。有罪の反対が無罪ではないのは, 陪審裁判では必ず合理的疑いをこえて (beyond a reasonable doubt) 有罪と認められるかどうかを判断するように求められるからです。つまり, 有罪の反対は「有罪というには証拠が十分ではない」というだけで, 必ずしも無罪というわけではないのです。

Advanced Topic: Social Exclusion Hurts

To claim that humans are a profoundly social species is no overstatement. As we have seen in the previous sections, some people are even willing to go along with an obviously "wrong" majority just to be liked. Indeed, we not only need other people to survive as infants and children, but as adults we positively require other people to thrive. Accordingly, some researchers consider that people are equipped with a **need to belong** (Baumeister & Leary, 1995). It is for this reason that **social exclusion**, due to bullying, rejection or even ostracism, is one of the most injurious things that can happen to a person.

Williams, Cheung, and Choi (2000) designed a remarkably simple, yet powerful experiment to manipulate feelings of social exclusion in an online environment. The experiment involves assigning a participant to play a videogame of catch-ball (known as **Cyberball**) with a small group of other players. In fact, the other players are confederates or computer programs, but the participant is made to think that he or she is interacting with real people. In the control condition, the confederates share the ball with each other as well as the participant. In other words, the participant is included in the game. In the experimental condition, however, the participant is excluded from the game. The confederates share the ball amongst themselves, but never once throw it to the participant. Can you imagine how it feels to be a participant in this condition? Williams and colleagues assessed participants' mood and self-esteem using self-report measures. They found that social exclusion in Cyberball causes an extremely negative emotional experience.

The results make sense—social exclusion *hurts* us. But do we really feel pain when we are rejected, or do we just use the phrase "hurt" because it is a conventional way of referring to rejection? Williams teamed up with two neuroscientists to tackle this question (Eisenberger, Lieberman, & Williams, 2003). They used **functional magnetic resonance imaging** (**fMRI**) to look inside the brains of people as they were being excluded in a game of Cyberball. The researchers found perhaps one of the most reaffirming findings in modern social psychological research—the brain areas most active during this experience were nearly identical to the areas active during the experience of physical pain! In this way, the researchers established that being excluded hurts. In other words, although social pain does not cause us to spill blood, the pain of social exclusion is neurologically equivalent to the pain of being punched, kicked, or beaten.

But why does social exclusion hurt? When we are injured, pain tells us that something is going wrong, and directs our attention to the problem. As social exclusion is no less fatal to a social species than are physical injuries, feeling the sting of social exclusion appears to be an adaptive response.

下の方に手だけ見えているのが参加者です。Inclusion 条件（control 条件）では参加者の手にもボールがまわってきますが，exclusion 条件では参加者の手にボールがパスされることはありません。

Figure **7**-6. A screenshot from the Cyberball game. ［作成者（Kip D. Williams）の許可を得て掲載］

Need to Belong：**所属欲求**　集団から受け入れられたいという欲求のことを所属欲求といいます。所属というと日本語では組織などのことを想像しがちですが，ここでは家族や友人関係を含む広い意味で，何らかの集団に受け入れられることを指して所属という言葉が使われています。

Social Exclusion：**社会的排除（社会的排斥）**　他者から仲間外れにされることです。オストラシズム（ostracism）という用語を使っている文献もあります。

　代表的な研究の方法に本文で紹介した**サイバーボール課題**（**Cyberball**）があります。この課題では，実験の参加者は他の参加者とボール投げゲームをしていると思わせられます。ですが，実際は他の参加者はコンピュータプログラムで，実験の目的にあわせて参加者は仲間外れにされたり（誰からもボールをパスしてもらえなかったり），仲間に入れてもらったりします。興味のある方は下記の Cyberball のサイトを見てください。

　　　https://cyberball.wikispaces.com/

社会的排除に関するそれ以外の実験方法として，性格検査の結果として，あなたは将来対人関係に恵まれずに寂しい人生を送る傾向があるという虚偽のフィードバックをするという方法などがあります。

Functional Magnetic Resonance Imaging (fMRI)：**機能的磁気共鳴画像法**　人の脳活動を脳内の血流量をもとに画像化する方法のことです。正式名称は長いので，機能的MRI（または日本語でも単に fMRI）と略称だけで表記してあることも多いので覚えておくとよいでしょう。

References

Allport, F. H. (1920). The influence of the group upon association and thought. *Journal of Experimental Psychology, 3*, 159-182. doi: 10.1037/h0067891

Asch, S. E. (1951). Effects of group pressure upon the modification and distortion of judgments. In H. Guetzkow (Ed.), *Groups, leadership and men* (pp. 177-190). Pittsburgh PA: Carnegie Press.

Asch, S. E. (1955). Opinions and social pressure. *Scientific American, 193*, 31-35. doi: 10.1038/scientificamerican1155-31

Baumeister, R. F., & Leary, M. R. (1995). The need to belong: Desire for interpersonal attachment as a fundamental human motivation. *Psychological Bulletin, 117*, 497-529. doi: 10.1037/0033-2909.117.3.497

Bond, C. F. Jr., & Titus, L. J. (1983). Social facilitation: A meta-analysis of 241 studies. *Psychological Bulletin, 94*, 265-292. doi: 10.1037/0033-2909.94.2.265

Deutsch, M., & Gerard, H. B. (1955). A study of normative and informational social influences upon individual judgment. *Journal of Abnormal and Social Psychology, 51*, 629-636. doi:10.1037/h0046408

Eisenberger, N. I., Lieberman, M. D., & Williams, K. D. (2003). Does rejection hurt? An fMRI study of social exclusion. *Science, 302*, 290-292. doi: 10.1126/science.1089134

Kalven, H., Jr., & Zeisel, H. (1966). *The American jury*. Boston: Little, Brown.

Latané, B. (1981). The psychology of social impact. *American Psychologist, 36*, 343-356. doi: 10.1037/0003-066X.36.4.343

Latané, B., Williams, K., & Harkins, S. (1979). Many hands make light the work: The causes and consequences of social loafing. *Journal of Personality and Social Psychology, 37*, 822-832. doi: 10.1037/0022-3514.37.6.822

Moscovici, S., Lage, E., & Naffrechoux, M. (1969). Influence of a consistent minority on the responses of a majority in a color perception task. *Sociometry, 32*, 365-380. doi: 10.2307/2786541

Nemeth, C. J. (1986). Differential contributions of majority and minority influence. *Psychological Review, 93*, 23-32. doi: 10.1037/0033-295X.93.1.23

Steiner, I. D. (1972). *Group process and productivity*. New York: Academic Press.

Triplett, N. (1898). The dynamogenic factors in pacemaking and competition. *American Journal of Psychology, 9*, 507-533. doi: 10.2307/1412188

Williams, K. D., Cheung, C. K. T., & Choi, W. (2000). Cyberostracism: Effects of being ignored over the Internet. *Journal of Personality and Social Psychology, 79*, 748-762. doi: 10.1037/0022-3514.79.5.748

Zajonc, R. B. (1965). Social facilitation. *Science, 149*, 269-274. doi: 10.1126/science.149.3681.269

CHAPTER 8

Intergroup Relations

集団間関係

8.1
The Power of Intergroup Situations

8.2
The Robbers Cave Experiment

8.3
Social Identity Theory

8.4
Cognition in Intergroup Contexts

8.5
Intergroup Contact Reduces Prejudice

Advanced Topic
Are There Hidden Forms of Racism?

8.1 The Power of Intergroup Situations

Intergroup situations are extremely common and sometimes exert a strong influence upon us—often much stronger than we expect. When you were a kid at elementary school, did your school have a Sports Day (*undo-kai*)? If so, you were likely divided into red and white teams for no obvious reason. Since the teams were randomly generated, it shouldn't have mattered who won or lost. However, you likely felt good when your teammates (some of whom were not even your friends) performed better than the opposing team.

Fortunately, Sports Day teams are typically not of any major consequence. But what happens if you instill people with the vicious idea that one group is inherently superior to another? This was actually done by an American schoolteacher Jane Elliott[1] in response to the assassination of Martin Luther King, Jr.[2] In her now-classic experiment, documented on film in 1970, she taught her 3rd graders an invaluable lesson about the evils of **prejudice** and **discrimination** against so-called "colored[3]" people.

Over the course of two days, Mrs. Elliott created a situation in which all of her students would experience what it feels like to be both the victim *and* the perpetrator of discrimination. On the first day she informed all of her students that blue-eyed children were superior to brown-eyed children. She explained that brown-eyed children were less worthy than blue-eyed children, and imposed a series of discriminatory rules against them. For example, brown-eyed children weren't allowed to use the water fountain just outside the classroom, they weren't allowed to play with blue-eyed children on the playground, and they had to come in from recess five minutes earlier than the blue-eyed children. Naturally, the blue-eyed children enjoyed their superiority, and they began to pick on the brown-eyed children using insults such as "brown-eyes!" By contrast, the brown-eyed children began to internalize their problems as a result of their brown eyes. When one child was asked what it means to be called "brown-eyes," he responded, "It means that we're stupid."

On the second day of the lesson, Mrs. Elliott reversed the situation. She informed her class that she had lied, and that in fact, brown-eyed children were superior to blue-eyed children. She reversed the rules, and throughout the second day, she belittled the blue-eyed children. Within the course of one day, the attitudes of the brown-eyed children changed dramatically. They were more positive and performed better during the second day. By comparison, blue-eyed children had a very bad second day.

After the lesson, Mrs. Elliott **debriefed** the children. They had learned not only that it is bad to judge people on the basis of the color of their eyes, but that it is, by extension, bad to judge people by the color of their skin. Why, then, do intergroup contexts exert such dramatic influence on our attitudes and behaviors? In this chapter, you will learn about social psychological studies that attempt to answer this all-important question.

Prejudice and **Discrimination**：偏見・差別　　偏見と差別は，日常的には同じような意味で用いますが，社会心理学では偏見と差別を感情と行動の区別に対応させて使います。

　偏見は，特定の集団の人たちに対して，その集団の成員だという理由でネガティヴな（非好意的な）感情をもつことを指します。

　差別は，特定の集団の人たちを，その集団の成員だという理由だけで平等に扱わないことです。

　ステレオタイプは，Section 3.3 で確認したように，特定の集団の人たちに対する紋切り型の見方（認知）です。ステレオタイプは必ずしもネガティヴなものとは限りません。

Debriefing：デブリーフィング　　辞書で debrief を引くと，（帰還した兵士などから）聞き取りをするというような意味が出てきます。Elliott の実験の場合，子どもたちは，午後のクラスルームの時間に目の色で分けられたことについてどう感じたか，意見を出し合っています。

　心理学では参加者への事後のインタビューも含めて，実験の主旨，ディセプションが含まれていればその内容について説明し，参加者に理解してもらう手続きをデブリーフィングといいます。

1　Jane Elliott（ジェーン・エリオット）の実験の様子は，ドキュメンタリーが作成されていて DVD（*A Class Divided*）で観ることができます。
2　Martin Luther King, Jr.：マーティン・ルーサー・キング・ジュニア　　日本ではキング牧師といわれることが多い公民権運動家です。フルネームもぜひ覚えてください。
3　Colored：有色の　　かつて，白人以外の人たちを表すために使われていた言葉です。また，colored（または colored people）として有色人種（特に黒人）を意味していました。現在では，肌の色に基づく偏見・差別に関連する使われ方はしませんが，偏った物の見方を意味する形容詞で使われることはあります（つまり，日本語の「色眼鏡」に近い使い方です）。

8.2 The Robbers Cave Experiment

Groups often fight against each other very aggressively, the extreme manifestation being war or even genocide. To help decipher the causes of, and solutions to, intergroup conflict, Sherif et al. (1961) ran an elaborate field experiment. They made use of a common children's activity in the United States, summer camp. First, they divided 22 eleven- to twelve-year-old boys, who had not previously met, into two groups so that the groups were equivalent in terms of the members' height, weight, etc. The boys then took part in a three-week summer camp, which the researchers designed to test a number of hypotheses regarding intergroup relations. This three-stage experiment (1 stage ≈ 1 week) is called the **Robbers Cave Experiment** after the name of the campsite.

In the first stage, the boys engaged in various cooperative group activities, such as hiking and swimming, with other group members, all the while unaware that another group was camping and participating in identical activities elsewhere at the same campsite. The first week of the summer camp acted to develop **ingroup** bonding. Toward the end of this stage, the boys even thought up names for their groups (the Eagles and the Rattlers).

In the second stage, the researchers introduced the groups to each other, and created a series of *real conflicts* over valued resources (e.g., a trophy, medals) by having the two groups play a series of competitive games, such as baseball and tug-of-war. This no doubt increased tension between the groups. What started out with simple name calling at lunch, eventually led to more severe behaviors. For example, after the Eagles were defeated by the Rattlers in a tug-of-war event, the Eagles took down the Rattlers' flag and set it on fire. By the end of the second stage, the boys had formed extremely negative images of their **outgroup** members. When asked to indicate their friends in the campsite, the boys chose outgroup members as friends less than 10% of the time (Figure 8-1).

In the third and final stage of the experiment, to reduce conflict, the researchers introduced **superordinate goals** that required the effort of both groups to achieve. For example, the researchers artificially created a problem with the camp's water supply, and announced that they needed both groups to cooperate to locate the leakage. Another problem required the groups to pool money for a movie that was prohibitively expensive for just one group to afford. In another instance, the groups joined forces to pull an apparently broken-down truck out of a rut. As shown in Figures 8-1 and 8-2, by the end of the third stage, conflict between groups had been substantially reduced. The boys even agreed to go back home all together on one bus. In this way, Sherif et al. provided support for **Realistic Conflict Theory**: *Intergroup conflicts arise when there is competition for limited resources*. Accordingly, when groups become dependent upon each other to achieve superordinate, common goals, conflict is reduced.

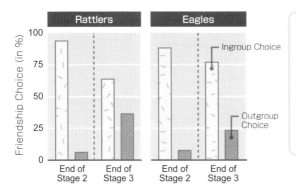

Figure 8-1. Friendship choice from each group. [Sherif et al., 1961]

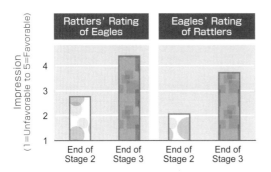

Figure 8-2. Mean impression measured by six items (brave, tough, friendly, sneaky*, smart alecs*, stinkers*) of the outgroup members at the end of stage 2 and the end of stage 3. [Sherif et al., 1961 より筆者作成]

Robbers Cave Experiment：泥棒洞窟実験　　この実験は，今でも**現実的葛藤理論**（**realistic conflict theory**）を支持する実証研究として頻繁に引用されています。

この実験では，サマーキャンプに参加した少年たちを2グループに分け，トロフィーなどの賞品のかかった野球や綱引きで繰り返し競争させることにより集団間葛藤を生起させました。その後，2グループが協力しないと解決できない問題を発生させることで，共通の**上位目標**（**superordinate goal**）を与えました。その結果，集団間の関係は改善しました。サマーキャンプを利用した実験なので，サマーキャンプ実験と呼ばれることもあります。

Figure 8-1には同じキャンプ地にいる少年たちから友人を選ばせた結果です。Stage 2の終了時にはお互い自分のグループ，つまり**内集団**（**ingroup**）だけを選ぶ傾向がありましたが，Stage 3の終了時には**外集団**（**outgroup**）からも友人を選んでいます。この結果は，Rattlersに顕著ですが，お互いの印象評定させた平均値（Figure 8-2）で見ると両グループで改善が見られていることがわかります。

CHAPTER **8**　Intergroup Relations

8.3 Social Identity Theory

In the late 1960s, Tajfel questioned whether real conflicts over scarce resources are absolutely necessary for intergroup conflict to arise. Tajfel, Billig, Bundy, and Flament (1971) subsequently tested this idea developing the so-called **minimal group paradigm**, whereby participants are divided into two groups based on some trivial criterion, such as whether you tend to overestimate or underestimate the number of dots displayed on a screen (Tajfel et al.'s Experiment 1), or which of two stylistically-similar modern artists' (Klee's or Kandinsky's) paintings you select as more appealing (Experiment 2). In both experiments, participants are only informed of their own group membership (e.g., you are an "overestimator" or "Klee fan"), and do not interact with other group members face-to-face. In this way, groups are formed based on a minimal condition (i.e., trivial categorization). Even in such an artificial setting, when asked to determine the amount of rewards/penalties for ingroup and outgroup members, participants demonstrate **ingroup favoritism**—treating their ingroup members more favorably than outgroup members.

Based on this finding, Tajfel and Turner (1979) developed **social identity theory**. According to this theory, people derive part of their self-image from their social groups, and "strive to achieve or to maintain positive social identity" (p. 40) because this identity improves self-esteem. Moreover, Tajfel and Turner surmised that social identity is enhanced by favorable comparisons of one's "superior" ingroup to an "inferior" outgroup.

Aside from the minimal group setting, another interesting, related phenomenon—**basking in reflected glory**—evinces that people use social group membership to bolster their self-esteem. In a field study conducted in their psychology classes, Cialdini and colleagues counted the number of students who wore clothes identifying their school during the university football season (Cialdini et al., 1976). As shown in Figure 8-3, students were more likely to wear clothes identifying their school after their school football team won a game. Cialdini et al. also conducted the following, rather clever, study: In a telephone survey, respondents first answered several factual questions about their university. They then received feedback that they performed better/worse than average on the questions. Respondents were finally asked to describe one of their football team's winning/losing games. The researchers simply counted the frequency with which respondents used "we" to describe the winning/losing game. As shown in Figure 8-4, the pronoun "we" was more frequently used to describe the winning game (e.g., "We won"). This tendency was especially pronounced when respondents had previously received a failure feedback. It is as if respondents tried to compensate for their damaged self-esteem by emphasizing their positive social identity.

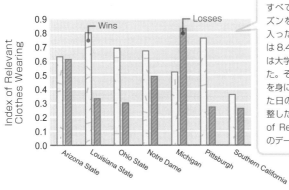

Figure 8-3. Mean index of wearing clothes identifying one's school.［Cialdini et al., 1976 より筆者作成］

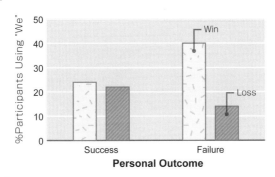

Figure 8-4. Percentage of participants who used "we" to describe their team's winning/losing game as a function of the feedback they received on an unrelated task (success vs. failure).［Cialdini et al., 1976 より筆者作成］

Minimal Group Paradigm：最小条件集団パラダイム　　Tajfel et al. (1971) は，現実的葛藤理論では偏見や差別の原因をすべて説明することはできないと考えて，現実的な葛藤のまったくない集団（最小条件集団）を作り，そこでも**内集団ひいき**（**ingroup favoritism**）が観察されることを示しました。

Social Identity Theory：社会的アイデンティティ理論　　社会的アイデンティティ理論では，自分がある集団に所属しているという事実は，自己のアイデンティティの一部を構成すると考えます。そして，集団への所属に基づくアイデンティティを社会的アイデンティティと呼んでいます。

Basking in Reflected Glory（**BIRGing**）：栄光浴　　BIRGingとは反対に失敗した集団と関わらないようにすることをCutting off Reflected Failure (CORFing) といいます。例えば，応援しているスポーツチームが負けると，そのチームのポスターをはがしてしまうことなどが例として挙げられます。

CHAPTER **8**　Intergroup Relations

8.4 Cognition in Intergroup Contexts

We saw in previous chapters on the self (CHAPTER 2) and social cognition (CHAPTER 3) that our perceptions of reality are sometimes distorted in a self-serving way. So, you probably won't be surprised to know that our perceptions of reality are also distorted in favor of our ingroups. A classic study on this topic was conducted at Dartmouth College and Princeton University following their football teams' clash in the final game of the 1951 season (Hastorf & Cantril, 1954). Early in the game, Princeton's star quarterback (their "idol") was benched for a broken nose, and later, in what could be seen as retaliation, Dartmouth's quarterback was benched for a broken leg. After the tumultuous game, the researchers noted that their campus newspapers reported quite different stories. Princeton's newspaper read "Both teams were guilty but the blame must be laid primarily on Dartmouth's doorstep," while Dartmouth's newspaper read "When an idol is hurt there is only one recourse—the tag of dirty football." It is as if both sides watched different games!

A week later, students at each school watched a film of the game, and reported any infractions of the rules they saw. As shown in Figure 8-5, Dartmouth students reported a near equal number of infractions committed by both teams (despite their team having committed slightly more infractions), while Princeton students reported that their opponent committed over twice as many infractions. Thus, students' perceptions of an identical event, were distorted in favor of their own groups.

Another well-known cognitive bias in the intergroup context is the **outgroup homogeneity effect**—we tend to see outgroup members as alike, while seeing ingroup members as more individual. For example, you might think that most Germans love beer, or most French love wine. But if you hear someone say "most Japanese love *sake*," you might say "No! That's not true." If you feel this way, perhaps you see outgroup members (Germans or French) as more homogeneous than ingroup members (Japanese).

In one study, researchers had participants estimate the proportion of men/women who would endorse several gender-specific stereotypical statements (Park & Rothbart, 1982). Examples of masculine and feminine statements were "Even when I need help, I dislike accepting it from other people," and "I am afraid of snakes, rodents, and spiders," respectively. The results are shown in Figure 8-6. The left panel indicates that male participants inferred that females are homogeneous—that most women would endorse feminine but not masculine statements. Female participants' estimates were not quite as extreme as the males'. This result is evidenced by a steeper dark than light line. When men were the target (the right panel of Figure 8-6), however, women were more extreme in their estimations (the steeper light line in the right panel). In this way, both men and women exhibited some degree of the outgroup homogeneity bias.

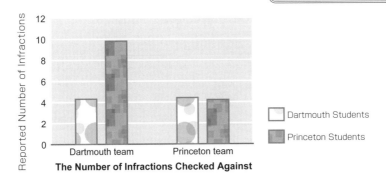

Figure 8-5. The number of infractions reported by Dartmouth/Princeton students for the Dartmouth/Princeton teams.［Hastorf & Cantril, 1954 より筆者作成］

本文でこのグラフの傾斜が急であることが外集団等質性効果があることを示していると書いています。このことを左側の図（女性に対するステレオタイプの図）で確認してみましょう。Stereotypicで値が大きいことは，女性のステレオタイプ的な特徴がより多くの女性に当てはまると考えていることを示しています。一方 counter-stereotypic の値が小さいことは，男性のステレオタイプ的特徴が当てはまる女性がほとんどいないと考えていることを示しています。つまり，ほとんどの女性は女性的な特徴をもち，男性的な特徴をもっていないという判断パターンは急な右下がりのラインとなります。

Figure 8-6. The estimated proportion of group members who endorse items as a function of gender of participants and gender of target group.［Park & Rothbart, 1982］

Outgroup Homogeneity Effect（outgroup homogeneity bias）：**外集団等質性効果**　自分自身の集団（内集団）の成員には個性がありいろいろな人がいると思うのに対して，外集団の人たちは同じような人たちだと見なす傾向のことです。

CHAPTER **8**　Intergroup Relations

8.5 Intergroup Contact Reduces Prejudice

In this chapter, we have seen how easily people can become trapped in mutual hostility or ingroup favoritism in intergroup situations. While many researchers have devoted their time and effort to understanding how intergroup conflicts arise, other researchers have devoted their energy to understanding how to reduce intergroup conflicts. One of the most famous hypotheses is the so-called **contact hypothesis** (also known as contact theory or intergroup contact theory), proposed by Gordon Allport more than half a century ago in his book *The Nature of Prejudice* (Allport, 1954). According to the contact hypothesis, contact between groups under favorable conditions, such as equal status and the presence of common goals, reduces prejudice.

Although some people liked the contact hypothesis, others considered it simply too optimistic. In fact, some authors argued that contact between hostile groups actually adds fuel to the fire. In the Robbers Cave Experiment, for example, simply having lunch together at the same place led the Eagles and Rattlers to partake in name calling and other nasty behaviors (see Section 8.2). Thus, putting two opposing groups together does not necessarily reduce prejudice. In other words, researchers have accumulated evidence both *for* and *against* the contact hypothesis.

Fortunately, in this situation there is a means to adequately integrate conflicting evidence in an objective manner—**meta-analysis**. Two social psychologists, Pettigrew and Tropp (2006), located 515 papers that report the effect of intergroup contact on prejudice. The 515 papers included 1,383 empirical effects; some were supportive of the hypothesis and some were not. Nonetheless, by statistically weighting all 1,383 effects, Pettigrew and Tropp showed that intergroup contact, on average, reduces prejudice. The average **effect size** (measured by a correlation coefficient) across these studies is approximately −.20. Therefore we can conclude that intergroup contact is moderately effective at reducing prejudice. In this meta-analysis, Pettigrew and Tropp also revealed that the effect of contact reduces prejudice toward various types of groups (e.g., groups defined by ethnicity, sexual orientation, age, and physical/mental disabilities).

In a follow-up meta-analysis, Pettigrew and Tropp (2008) investigated the factors that **mediate** the effect of intergroup contact. The results are shown in Figure 8−7. First, intergroup contact reduces prejudice by reducing *anxiety* toward outgroup members. Second, intergroup contact heightens *empathy* toward outgroup members, possibly because intergroup contact creates a situation in which one can more easily take the perspective of the outgroup members. This heightened empathy then reduces prejudice.

Admitting that negative intergroup contact can make things worse, positive intergroup contact seems to effectively reduce intergroup prejudice.

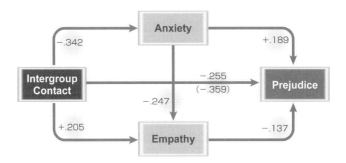

Figure 8-7. The results of a path model. The effect of intergroup contact on prejudice was partially mediated by anxiety and empathy. [Pettigrew & Tropp, 2008]

Contact Hypothesis：接触仮説　外集団に対する偏見は，相手のグループについて知ることで（接触することで）低減するという考え方です。

Meta-analysis：メタ分析　過去に行われた研究の結果を集め，それを統計的に再分析する手法のことです（Section 7.1 の補足 4 も参照）。この分析では，それぞれの研究で報告されている**効果量**（**effect size**）を集めます。接触仮説に関していうと，効果量とは，接触の有無によって偏見がどれくらい減るかを一般的な指標で表したものです。例えば，本文中では効果量（r）が − .20 と見積もられたと述べています。Al Ramiah & Hewstone（2013）によれば，この効果量（接触と偏見の関係の強さ）は，受動喫煙と肺がんの関係の強さとだいたい同じくらいということです。

Mediation：媒介　ある要因が，結果に直接影響するのではなく，別のもの（M）に影響し，その影響を介して間接的に結果に影響しているときに（要因→ M →結果），M が要因と結果を媒介しているといいます。

CHAPTER **8**　Intergroup Relations

Advanced Topic: Are There Hidden Forms of Racism?

Racism may seem to be a relic of the past in many parts of the United States of America. Most white Americans no longer support racial segregation; no longer say things like "I would move if a black family moved to my neighborhood." However, many people consider that other, less obvious, forms of racism such as **symbolic racism** still remain.

For example, some implicit tests, such as the Implicit Association Test (IAT), indicate that a substantial portion of white Americans still carry some negative image of black Americans (see Advanced Topic of CHAPTER 6). Likewise, can you guess what happened when a group of neuroscientists scanned white Americans' brain activity while watching white and black faces (Phelps et al., 2000)? They were particularly interested in a small almond-shaped brain area, the **amygdala**, which many studies have implicated in the emotional reaction of fear. Participants' amygdala activation tended to be slightly greater when they were watching black faces than white faces, yet due to substantial individual differences, this tendency was not significant. More importantly, however, the individual differences in amygdala activation were significantly correlated with participant's IAT scores: Those who were judged as having greater pro-white implicit attitudes also tended to have greater amygdala activation when viewing black-versus-white faces (see Figure 8-8). Nevertheless, the individual differences in amygdala activation were not correlated with responses to self-report (explicit) measures of racism.

You might ask why be bothered by this brain response if it doesn't relate to self-reported racism. Indeed, some research shows that exposure to black faces activates brain regions associated with emotion regulation: It seems that many biased people actively regulate their implicit negative racial bias (see Kubota, Banaji, & Phelps, 2012, for a review). If these people are successful, implicit negative attitudes won't cause any consequential problems. But what if such negative attitudes influence our judgments and behaviors at the unconscious level?

In a study conducted by Payne (2001), participants were shown a picture of a white or black man followed by a photo of either a gun or a tool. The task was to simply categorize the object as a gun or tool. As expected, participants were faster to respond to guns that were preceded by black faces, indicating a stronger association between guns and black faces. In a second study, Payne forced participants to respond very quickly (within 500 milliseconds). In this study, participants made more mistakes of categorizing a tool as a gun after being exposed to a black face (see Figure 8-9). Considering these findings, think again about the central question posed by this section. How do you answer?

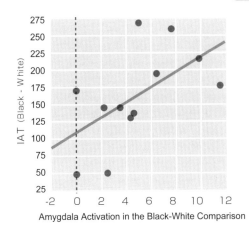

Figure 8-8. Correlation between the magnitude of amygdala activation to black versus-white faces and the IAT response latency for black–white. ($r = .576$) [Phelps et al., 2000]

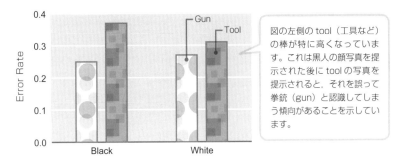

Figure 8-9. Error rate as a function of the primed photograph (black vs. white) and target stimulus (gun vs. tool). [Payne, 2001 より筆者作成]

Symbolic Racism：象徴的人種差別主義　　以前ほど露骨ではない人種差別主義のことをこのようにいいます。また，主に社会心理学で，これを modern racism（現代的人種差別主義）ということがあります。

Amygdala：扁桃核（扁桃体）

References

Allport, G. W. (1954). *The nature of prejudice*. Cambridge, MA: Addison-Wesley.

Al Ramiah, A., & Hewstone, M. (2013). Intergroup contact as a tool for reducing, resolving, and preventing intergroup conflict: Evidence, limitations, and potential. *American Psychologist, 68*, 527-542. doi: 10.1037/a0032603

Cialdini, R. B., Borden, R. J., Thorne, A., Walker, M. R., Freeman, S., & Sloan, L. R. (1976). Basking in reflected glory: Three (football) field studies. *Journal of Personality and Social Psychology, 34*, 366-375. doi: 10.1037/0022-3514.34.3.366

Hastorf, A. H., & Cantril, H. (1954). They saw a game: A case study. *Journal of Abnormal and Social Psychology, 49*, 129-134. doi: 10.1037/h0057880

Kubota, J. T., Banaji, M. R., & Phelps, E. A. (2012). The neuroscience of race. *Nature Neuroscience, 15*, 940-948. doi: 10.1038/nn.3136

Park. B., & Rothbart, M. (1982). Perception of out-group homogeneity and levels of social categorization: Memory for the subordinate attributes of in-group and out-group members. *Journal of Personality and Social Psychology, 42*, 1051-1068. doi: 10.1037/0022-3514.42.6.1051

Payne, B. K. (2001). Prejudice and perception: The role of automatic and controlled processes in misperceiving a weapon. *Journal of Personality and Social Psychology, 81*, 181-192. doi: http://dx.doi.org/10.1037/0022-3514.81.2.181

Pettigrew, T. F., & Tropp, L. R. (2006). A meta-analytic test of intergroup contact theory. *Journal of Personality and Social Psychology, 90*, 751-783. doi: 10.1037/0022-3514.90.5.751

Pettigrew, T. F., & Tropp, L. R. (2008). How does intergroup contact reduce prejudice? Meta-analytic tests of three mediators. *European Journal of Social Psychology, 38*, 922-934. doi: 10.1002/ejsp.504

Phelps, E. A., O'Connor, K. J., Cunningham, W. A., Funayama, E. S., Gatenby, J. C., Gore, J. C., & Banaji, M. R. (2000). Performance on indirect measures of race evaluation predicts amygdala activation. *Journal of Cognitive Neuroscience, 12*, 729-738. doi: 10.1162/089892900562552

Sherif, M., Harvey, O. J., White, B. J., Hood, W. R., & Sherif, C. W. (1961). *Intergroup conflict and cooperation: The Robbers Cave experiment*. Norman, OK: University (of Oklahoma) Book Exchange.

Tajfel, H., Billig, M. G., Bundy, R. P., & Flament, C. (1971). Social categorization and intergroup behaviour. *European Journal of Social Psychology, 1*, 149-178. doi: 10.1002/ejsp.2420010202

Tajfel, H., & Turner, J. (1979). An integrative theory of intergroup conflict. In W. G. Austin & S. Worchel (Eds.), *The social psychology of intergroup relations* (pp. 33-47). Monterey, CA: Brooks-Cole.

CHAPTER 9

Prosocial Behavior

向社会的行動

9.1
Situational Influence on Prosocial Behavior

9.2
The Empathy-Altruism Hypothesis

9.3
The Murder of Kitty Genovese and Unresponsive Bystanders

9.4
The Bystander Effect and Diffusion of Responsibility

Advanced Topic
Punishment and Cooperation

9.1 Situational Influence on Prosocial Behavior

Most world religions emphasize **altruism** (or **prosocial behavior** more broadly). Christianity is no exception. Have you ever heard the parable of the Good Samaritan[1]? It starts out with a traveler who has been beaten and left to die in the road. No one is willing to help him. Even some religious people ignore his suffering and continue on their way. Fortunately, a Samaritan (i.e., a person from the land of Samaria) eventually comes by, and generously helps the traveler, thereby saving his life. This story was used by Jesus Christ as an example of how Christians should love their neighbors no matter what.

If religion teaches the importance of altruism, we might expect religious people to act rather helpfully toward people in need. Darley and Batson (1973) tested this claim. They first contacted students at a theological seminary[2], and assessed their personality and religiosity. The researchers then asked participants to come to the laboratory to take part in a study concerning the vocational careers of seminary students. When participants arrived at the laboratory, they were tasked with giving a brief speech in a different building. The importance of altruism was made **salient** for half of the participants by asking them to give a speech about the parable of the Good Samaritan. The other half were asked to give a speech about the future careers of seminary students. Once participants understood the instructions, they were then asked to go to another building where an assistant was waiting for them. When providing directions to the room, the experimenter said either one of three things according to the condition to which the participant was assigned: "Oh, you're late... you'd better hurry..." in the high-hurry condition, "The assistant is ready for you" in the intermediate-hurry condition, and "It'll be a few minutes before they're ready for you" in the low-hurry condition.

When passing through an alley en route to their destination, participants encountered a person sitting alone who apparently needed help. However, he was, in fact, a confederate. The researchers were interested in whether the seminary students would offer help to this person in need. Overall, 40% of the participants (16/40) offered some form of help (e.g., directly asking if he needed help; notifying the assistant about the person). So, what do you think predicted this helping behavior? Personality variables did not. The salience of altruism (whether participants were to talk about the Good Samaritan or future careers) also did not. The only statistically significant predictor of helping behavior was whether students were in a hurry. As shown in Figure 9-1, 63% of students helped when they were not in a hurry, but only 10% did so when they were in a hurry. Therefore, the results clearly show that even highly religious students are subject to situational influences when deciding whether or not to help someone in need. In other words, prosocial behavior can be determined by external factors, and is amenable to experimental research.

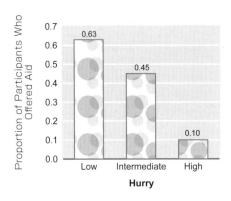

Figure 9-1. Proportion of participants who offered aid to the confederate as a function of the hurry condition.［Darley & Batson, 1973 より筆者作成］

Altruism：利他主義，利他性／**Prosocial Behavior**：向社会的行動（順社会的行動）
向社会的行動はいわゆる「よい行い」全般を指します。他者の福利を向上させるためにとられる利他行動（altruistic behavior）は，向社会的行動に含まれます（CHAPTER 1 の Advanced Topic でも説明しています）。

Salient：（対象となるものの）**顕現性が高い**（この文脈では利他主義の重要性に思い至りやすい状態にあるという意味です）

> 補足6　この Darley & Batson の実験は，性格などの個人差変数が行動と相関しないという主張の論拠としてしばしば引用されます。しかし，この実験に参加したのが全員神学校の学生だったということに注意してください。つまり，宗教性が非常に高い人ばかりが実験に参加していたということです。もしかすると，普通の大学生が実験参加者であったなら（宗教性がとても低い人からとても高い人までが実験に参加していたなら），宗教性と援助行動の間に相関が見られていたかもしれません。

1　Parable of the Good Samaritan：善きサマリア人のたとえ　どのような人が愛すべき隣人かと尋ねられたときにキリストが語ったたとえ話を指しています。
2　Seminary：神学校

9.2 The Empathy-Altruism Hypothesis

Although this chapter deals with prosocial behaviors, do people really engage in them out of an altruistic motivation? Many philosophers think the answer is NO. You might offer your seat to an elderly person on the bus, but perhaps you don't care about the well-being of the elderly, and care only about your public image. Therefore, an egoistic motivation can cause an altruistic behavior. So, is there any evidence that people can possess a genuinely altruistic motivation? This is a deep philosophical question, isn't it? However, for social psychologists, this is an empirical question, one that can be answered with an experiment.

Batson noted that altruistic motivation should be other-regarding (i.e., directed toward someone else's well-being). Because empathy is considered an other-regarding emotion, Batson hypothesized that empathy would foster a genuinely altruistic motivation—the **empathy-altruism hypothesis** (Batson, Duncan, Ackerman, Buckley, & Birch, 1981).

To test this hypothesis, Batson and colleagues had two female participants enter a laboratory. One of them (named Elaine) was actually a confederate. The participant, who had filled out a personal values and interests questionnaire prior to the experiment, was then given a copy of Elaine's questionnaire. As a part of the experimental manipulation, the participant learned that Elaine had either similar or dissimilar values and interests. (It is known that people readily empathize with similar others, but not so easily with dissimilar others.) The participant was next asked to observe Elaine receive a series of electric shocks as part of a supposed memory recall task. Although the shocks delivered to Elaine were mild, she exhibited an extremely painful reaction. Elaine explained that she had trauma regarding electric shocks. At this point, the experimenter asked the participant if she would be willing to replace Elaine and receive the remaining electric shocks in her place. To distinguish genuine altruistic behavior from altruistic behavior driven by egoistic motivation (i.e., "selfish" altruism), half of the participants were free to leave, while the other half were made to observe Elaine until all shocks had been administered.

The results are shown in Figure 9-2. As Batson predicted, when participants did not empathize with Elaine, whether they helped her hinged upon whether or not it was easy to escape the situation (see the left side of Figure 9-2). The low empathy participants just cared about their own feelings, and escaped as soon as they got the chance. If the low empathy participants had to stay, however, they helped, but only because observing someone's extremely painful responses is distressing. On the other hand, when participants felt empathy with Elaine, they helped her even when escape was easy (see the right side of Figure 9-2)! This experiment clearly shows that at least some helping behaviors are driven by a genuinely altruistic motivation.

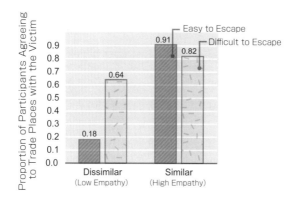

Figure 9-2. Proportion of participants who agreed to trade places with Elaine (the victim) as a function of similarity with the victim and difficulty to escape from the situation. [Batson et al., 1981 より筆者作成]

Empathy-Altruism Hypothesis：共感・利他性仮説　共感した相手に対しては，相手の福利を気にかけ，相手の福利を向上させることを目的として（真に利他的な動機に基づき）行動することがあるという仮説です。

　ここで，利他的な動機に基づかない利他行動（エゴイスティックな利他行動）には，自己のイメージを気にした利他行動や，自分自身の苦痛を取り除くための利他行動が含まれます。

　Batson et al. (1981) の実験には，Elaine を見続けることで自分自身が苦しい思いをするという前提があります。ですから，その苦痛を取り除くために Elaine の代わりに自分で電気ショックを受けようとすることはエゴイスティックな利他行動とされています。

　よい評判を獲得するためにとられる利他行動については CHAPTER 1 の Advanced Topic で紹介している Simpson & Willer (2008) の実験も参考にして下さい。

9.3 The Murder of Kitty Genovese and Unresponsive Bystanders

Around 3 a.m. on March 13th, 1964, a lady named Kitty Genovese was raped and murdered just outside her apartment in New York City. It was a gruesome murder, but not markedly more so than other murders in New York City at the time. Nonetheless, a newspaper article written by Martin Gansberg (1964) transformed the murder case into one of the most memorable in history. The article described an eerie fact of the murder: While Genovese was being raped and killed, at least 38 law-abiding[1] neighbors heard her multiple screams for help, yet only one person called the police. And this call wasn't even made until over half an hour later, well after everyone heard her first scream. The title of Gansberg's article was "37 Who Saw Murder Didn't Call the Police." The subtitle of the article is also telling: "Apathy at Stabbing of Queens Woman Shocks Inspector.[2]" As this subtitle suggests, many people were disturbed by the unresponsiveness of these New Yorkers. Naturally, many readers felt perplexed and wondered why no one called the police much earlier. If you feel the same way, you are not alone.

Two social psychologists, Latané and Darley, who became interested in the case, however, saw things from a decidedly different perspective. Notice that when you feel the same as the readers of the article, you are implicitly attributing the witnesses' behavior (i.e., not calling the police) to an internal cause (i.e., their apathy). Latané and Darley (1970), instead, suspected that an external cause (i.e., the situation), might better explain the unresponsiveness of the 37 witnesses.[3]

Thus, by closely examining the details of this tragic situation, they developed a five-step model to explain why people help, or as is all too often the case, fail to do anything at all. The model assumes that for helping behavior to occur, (1) a potential helper must pay *attention* to the incident, (2) he/she must *interpret* the situation adequately (i.e., that help is needed), (3) he/she must consider that he/she is *responsible* for helping the victim, (4) he/she must judge that he/she is *capable* of doing so, and (5) he/she must *decide* to do so. As many neighbors were awakened by Kitty's screams, all 38 witnesses passed the first step. However, some did not pass the second step; they considered the screams to be lovers' quarrels. Some claimed that they were not sure what was going on because it was dark outside. No doubt there was some ambiguity, which might have made the right interpretation difficult. However, the third step—on taking responsibility—was probably more important: because the witnesses saw the lights in their neighbors' windows, many came to believe that someone else had already called the police. One elderly lady even admitted that she stopped her husband from calling the police by reminding him that there probably had been dozens of calls already. In the next section, you will learn about some ingenious social psychological experiments that corroborated the importance of this essential, third step.

補足7 カップルのケンカだと思うと介入しないのか？

　　Some of the witnesses of Kitty Genovese's murder claimed they did not intervene because they thought it was a lovers' quarrel. This is consistent with the second step of Latané and Darley's model of helping behavior (i.e., an adequate interpretation is necessary for witnesses to help). However, do people really tend *not* to intervene in lovers' quarrels?

　　Shotland and Straw (1976) empirically tested this notion. When participants were filling out a questionnaire by themselves, they overheard a staged verbal argument between a man and a woman. Next, they heard a man physically attack a woman. In the control condition (the stranger condition), she shouted "get away from me. I don't know you." In the experimental condition (the married condition), she screamed loudly, "get away from me. I don't know why I ever married you." Whether participants would intervene was secretly observed.

　　In the control (stranger) condition, a full 65% of participants intervened. On the other hand, in the married condition (when participants thought that it was a lovers' quarrel), only 19% intervened. This result is consistent with Latané and Darley's model—interpretation matters.

1　law-abiding：法律をきちんと守る
2　Apathy：無関心　　他者に対する冷淡な反応以外に，political apathy（政治的無関心）のようにも使われます。また，このサブタイトルの中のQueensは，事件が発生したニューヨーク市クイーンズ区のことを指しています。
3　LatanéとDarleyの一連の研究は，*The Unresponsive Bystander: Why Doesn't He Help?* というタイトルの本としてまとめられています。これは『冷淡な傍観者——思いやりの社会心理学』として翻訳版が出版されていて，日本語でも読むことができます。

9.4 The Bystander Effect and Diffusion of Responsibility

Latané and Darley hypothesized that the presence of others (specifically, bystanders) would decrease the likelihood of intervention. This became known as the **bystander effect**. One important antecedent of the bystander effect is **diffusion of responsibility**: The presence of others dilutes each person's sense of responsibility for the distress of the victim, and as a result, decreases the likelihood of intervention. (Recall that we already learned about diffusion of responsibility in Section 7.2 as an antecedent of social loafing.)

In the first test of this hypothesis, Darley and Latané (1968) led participants to believe that they would interact with one vs. two vs. five other fellow students using state-of-the-art[1] technology, an intercom system. Each participant was ushered to a separate room. At the beginning of the experiment, the experimenter announced that for the purpose of anonymity he would not listen to their interactions. During the course of the experiment, one student (in fact, a recorded voice) suddenly started seeking help while apparently suffering from a seizure. As can be seen in Figure 9-3, when participants believed that they were the only person who was able to offer help, 85% of them reported the accident to the experimenter. However, this rate declined as the group size increased. This result clearly supports the diffusion of responsibility hypothesis. As there are more bystanders, each individual becomes less likely to offer help to the victim.[2]

Apart from this responsibility-diluting effect, bystanders also serve as a cue to interpret a situation. If they appear undisturbed in the face of someone's adversity, people may well interpret the situation as not so urgent. Latané and Rodin (1969) examined whether the presence of an unresponsive bystander would suppress helping behavior. They had their participants fill out a questionnaire either alone or with a confederate in the room. The female experimenter then left the room. Four minutes after she left the room, participants heard the experimenter climb a chair to take something from the top of a bookshelf. Then, she apparently fell down and screamed and moaned: "Oh, my God, my foot... I..., I can't move it. Oh... my ankle. I can't get this thing off me" (Latané & Rodin, 1969, p. 192). More than 70% of participants who were working alone offered help to the victim. However, when the confederate remained unresponsive to the scream, only 1 of 14 participants offered help! This is not attributable to the mere presence of "someone else." When two real participants simultaneously took part in this experiment, 40% of the pairs eventually offered help. If they were friends, 70% of the pairs did so. Thus, intervention rates for real pairs were markedly higher than when participants were paired with an unresponsive confederate. Presumably, participants underestimated the seriousness of the situation using the confederate's reaction (or lack thereof) as a situational cue.

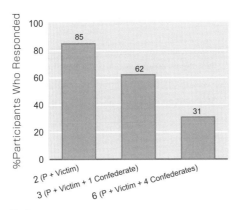

Figure **9**-3. Percentage of participants who responded to the emergency as a function of group size. ［Darley & Latané, 1968 より筆者作成］

Bystander Effect：傍観者効果　　援助が必要な場面（緊急事態）で，周りに自分と同じようにその様子を見ている人がいることで，一人ひとりの援助確率が低くなることをいいます。

Diffusion of Responsibility：責任の分散（Section 7.2 の説明を参照）

補足 8　傍観者効果とグループの援助確率

　　It is premature to conclude from Darley and Latané's (1968) result (shown in Figure 9-3) that a person is more likely to receive help when there is only one witness. In the six-person group, individual participants failed to respond to the emergency 69% of the time (= 100% − 31%). However, if each witness was a real participant, the probability that none of the five witnesses would intervene drops to just 16% (= $0.69^5 \times 100$). In other words, if you were in a six-person group and suffered from a seizure, you would be helped by at least one of the other five members 84% of the time (100% − 16%). Thus, this estimated probability that you would be helped if there were five real witnesses is approximately the same as the probability that Darley and Latané's hypothetical seizure victim was actually helped in the pair condition (85%, see the left bar in Figure 9-3).

1　State-of-the-art：最新式の　　ハイフンでつながった state-of-the-art 全体で形容詞として用います。
2　傍観者効果が子ども（5 歳児）でも見られることを示す研究もあります（Plötner, Over, Carpenter, & Tomasello, 2015）。

CHAPTER **9**　Prosocial Behavior　　115

Advanced Topic: Punishment and Cooperation

Aside from helping behavior, **cooperation** for the sake of the group is another form of prosocial behavior. For example, your community might periodically organize a litter pick-up. Such an activity keeps your neighborhood clean. However, you could be a free-rider—Even if you withheld participation, your neighbors would still clean up the area. This "**free-rider problem**" arises because a clean environment is a **public good**—anyone can benefit from it regardless of his/her own contribution. Interestingly, cooperation in such a public good situation is actually promoted by the presence of punishment. This effect was first documented by a Japanese social psychologist, Yamagishi (1986).

Yamagishi conducted an experiment mimicking the public good situation. As a member of an anonymous four-person group, participants repeatedly made a decision of how much of their 100 yen endowment they would contribute to other group members. If one participant contributes x yen, it would be doubled and equally divided among the other three group members (i.e., each of the other members would receive $2x/3$ yen). If no one in the group contributes anything, everyone would end up with the initial endowment of 100 yen. On the other hand, if everyone cooperates, everyone would receive 200 yen instead. Although cooperation may seem like the best strategy, there is an incentive to free-riding—if everyone else contributes 100 yen and you withhold (i.e., reserve your endowment), you get 300 yen. This is a standard public goods experiment. Here, however, Yamagishi introduced a so-called **sanction system**—the opportunity to punish the lowest contributor. If you contribute y yen to the sanction system, the lowest contributor in the original public good task would lose either y or $2y$ yen in the low and high sanction conditions, respectively.

The results are shown by the thick lines[1] in Figure 9-4. Although Yamagishi's analyses included another factor (participants' level of trusting others), let us focus on the effect of punishment here. The left-most panel shows the typical result under the no punishment condition: The cooperation rate declines over time (initial cooperators start withholding cooperation as they learn that others do not cooperate as much as themselves). The presence of punishment, however, increases the overall cooperation rate: 44.4%, 52.3%, and 74.1% in the control, low sanction, and high sanction conditions, respectively. Moreover, an efficient sanction system prevents the cooperation rate from declining (the right panel of Figure 9-4). Therefore, contribution to the sanction system is *instrumental* to sustain cooperation in the original (or *elementary*) public good situation.

Recently, experimental economists, Fehr and Gächter (2002), rediscovered this effect. They also found that people punish non-cooperators even when they will no longer interact with the same non-cooperators (thus punishment is non-instrumental). Accordingly, they coined the term **altruistic punishment**.

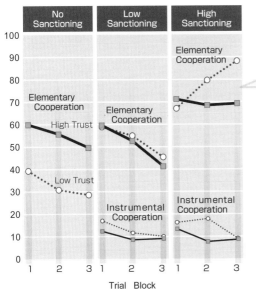

Figure 9-4. Cooperation rate (designated by thick lines) and punishment rate (designated by thin lines) as a function of the sanctioning system, trial block, and participants' level of trust. [Yamagishi, 1986]

Cooperation：協力

Free-rider Problem：ただ乗り問題（Section 7.2 も参照）

Public Good：公共財　経済学の用語で，いったんそこにあると誰もがそれから便益を受けることができる財を指します。例えば，公共の電波，公園，灯台などが公共財に含まれます。

Sanction System：制裁システム　悪い行いへの罰だけでなく，よい行いへの報酬も制裁に含めて考えることがあります。

Altruistic Punishment：利他的罰　罰された相手が将来の相互作用で協力するとしても，自分自身には利益はなく，将来の相互作用相手（他人）が利益を得るだけなので「利他的」罰といいます。直接被害にあっていない人（第三者）によって行使される場合，第三者罰（third-party punishment）という用語も使われます。

1　Figure 9-4 にはいろいろな種類の線が使われています。太い線と細い線がある場合，thick（太い），thin（細い）と表現することができます。実線と点線は solid line，dotted line のように表現することができます。

References

Batson, C. D., Duncan, B. D., Ackerman, P., Buckley, T., & Birch, K. (1981). Is empathic emotion a source of altruistic motivation? *Journal of Personality and Social Psychology, 40*, 290-302. doi: 10.1037/0022-3514.40.2.290

Darley, J. M., & Batson, C. D. (1973). "From Jerusalem to Jericho": A study of situational and dispositional variables in helping behavior. *Journal of Personality and Social Psychology, 27*, 100-108. doi: 10.1037/h0034449

Darley, J. M., & Latané, B. (1968). Bystander intervention in emergencies: Diffusion of responsibility. *Journal of Personality and Social Psychology, 8*, 377-383. doi: 10.1037/h0025589

Fehr, E., & Gächter, S. (2002). Altruistic punishment in humans. *Nature, 415*, 137-140. doi: 10.1038/415137a

Gansberg, M. (1964, March 24). 37 who saw murder didn't call the police. *The New York Times*. Retrieved from http://www.nytimes.com/1964/03/27/37-who-saw-murder-didnt-call-the-police.html?r=0

Latané, B., & Darley, J. M. (1970). *The unresponsive bystander: Why doesn't he help?* Englewood Cliffs, NJ: Prentice-Hall. (ラタネ, B. & ダーリー J. M. 竹村研一・杉崎和子 (訳) (1997).『冷淡な傍観者——思いやりの社会心理学』新装版, ブレーン出版)

Latané, B., & Rodin, J. (1969). A lady in distress: Inhibiting effects of friends and strangers on bystander intervention. *Journal of Experimental Social Psychology, 5*, 189-202. doi: 10.1016/0022-1031(69)90046-8

Plötner, M., Over, H., Carpenter, M., & Tomasello, M. (2015). Young children show the bystander effect in helping situations. *Psychological Science, 26*, 499-506. doi: 10.1177/0956797615569579

Shotland, R. L. & Straw, M. K. (1976). Bystander response to an assault: When a man attacks a woman. *Journal of Personality and Social Psychology, 34*, 990-999. http://dx.doi.org/10.1037/0022-3514.34.5.990

Yamagishi, T. (1986). The provision of a sanctioning system as a public good. *Journal of Personality and Social Psychology, 51*, 110-116. doi: 10.1037/0022-3514.51.1.110

CHAPTER 10

Antisocial Behavior

反社会的行動

10.1
Aggressive Behavior

10.2
Aggression Can Be Socially Learned

10.3
Obedience to Authority Ⅰ

10.4
Obedience to Authority Ⅱ

Advanced Topic
Long-term Effects of Media Violence

Supplementary Topic
The Stanford Prison Experiment

10.1 Aggressive Behavior

Harming others, or aggression, is a prominent form of antisocial behavior that has engaged scholarly interest from various disciplines including **psychoanalysis**, **ethology**, and social psychology. The first social psychological thesis about aggressive behavior, the **frustration-aggression hypothesis**, was proposed by a group of Yale psychologists (Dollard, Doob, Miller, Mowrer, & Sears, 1939). According to these psychologists, frustration, which is experienced when some goal-directed action or intention is blocked by external factors, "produces instigations to a number of different types of response, one of which is an instigation to some form of aggression" (Miller, 1941, p. 338).

One of the earliest pieces of evidence for the frustration-aggression hypothesis comes from real world data. From 1882 to 1930, during the specific years when economic conditions were bad (a cause of frustration), the number of lynchings in America (an extreme form of aggression) increased (Hovland & Sears, 1940). However, this negative correlation could be **spurious** due to two mutually independent trends that occurred during the studied period: a general decline in the number of lynchings and an overall increase in the value of cotton (an index of economic conditions). Nevertheless, the relationship remains even after the effects of these trends are removed (see Figure 10-1a for how to do this in the case of the number of lynchings): The number of lynchings (plotted upside-down in Figure 10-1b) still overlaps with the year-by-year value of cotton.

Despite some support for the frustration-aggression hypothesis, it contains a very strong assumption: "The occurrence of aggression always presupposes the existence of frustration" (Dollard et al., 1939, p. 1). This may not be tenable. For example, Geen (1968) had participants engage in a jigsaw puzzle in the following conditions. In the *task frustration condition*, participants worked on an unsolvable puzzle for five minutes. In the *personal frustration condition*, participants were given an easy puzzle but a confederate (putatively another participant) disturbed and prevented participants from solving the puzzle. Therefore, participants in these two conditions were not able to achieve their goal (i.e., solving the puzzle) and experienced frustration. In the *insult condition*, participants solved the puzzle (no frustration was experienced), however, the confederate delivered an insult to their intelligence. After these manipulations, participants were given a chance to deliver electric shocks of their chosen intensity to the confederate. Consistent with the frustration-aggression hypothesis, participants delivered greater shocks in the two frustration conditions than in a control condition that involved neither frustration nor insult. However, insulted participants also delivered stronger shocks to the confederate. Therefore, it is clear that insults, much like frustration, also cause aggression. In fact, a substantial portion of homicides are motivated by an altercation originating from insults or cursing (Wolfgang, 1958).

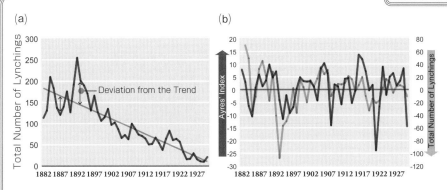

Figure **10**-1. (a) The number of lynchings in the U.S.A. from 1882 to 1930 and its trend (the declining straight line). The dual-headed arrows are examples of deviation scores. (b) Cotton value (Ayres' index) and the number of lynchings from 1882 to 1930. Both scores are adjusted against the trend (i.e., the deviation from the trend lines.)

> Figure 10-1 は Hovland & Sears (1940) に報告されているデータに基づき作成しました。その際，より直感的に理解しやすい Mintz (1946) による同データの再分析に即した図にしました。Hovland & Sears のデータについては，Hepworth & West (1988) も再分析を行い，結果の正しさが確認されています。

Psychoanalysis：精神分析（学）
Ethology：動物行動学（またはエソロジー）

Frustration-Aggression Hypothesis：フラストレーション・攻撃仮説　　Dollard et al. (1939) は，"the occurrence of aggression always presupposes the existence of frustration and, contrariwise, ...the existence of frustration always leads to some form of aggression" と述べています。著者のひとりの Neal Miller は，後半部分（フラストレーションは必ず攻撃につながる）は自分たちの意図したことではなかったと述べて，左ページのような修正表現を提案しています（Miller, 1941）。

Spurious Correlation：擬似相関　　本当は関係のない2つの事象が，それとは無関係な変数の影響であたかも関連しているように見えることを擬似相関といいます。本文の例に即していえば，リンチ事件の数と木綿の価値は19世紀後半から20世紀前半にかけてそれぞれ減少，上昇傾向であったので，本来関係がないとしても負の相関（一方が下がれば他方が上がる）という関係があるように見えてしまうということです。

　Hovland & Sears はリンチ事件数と木綿価値の関係が擬似相関ではないことを示すために，それぞれのデータから減少，上昇傾向の効果を取り除いた上で分析をしています。

10.2 Aggression Can Be Socially Learned

Not every aggression is caused by frustration (or insults). Many social psychologists accept the distinction between **hostile aggression**, harming someone for harm's sake, and **instrumental aggression**, harm which aims to achieve a desired goal (Feshbach, 1964). For example, a robber's goal is to obtain money, not terrorize people. Nevertheless, an aggressive behavior (e.g., stabbing someone with a knife) can be learned as an instrument to achieve one's goals (e.g., get money).

Social psychologist Bandura proposed the **social learning theory** of aggression. According to Bandura, people can learn to respond to certain situations aggressively by observing someone (a model) behave aggressively in a similar situation. In an early study (Bandura, Ross, & Ross, 1961), an experimenter invited a preschool child and an adult to play with toys in different corners of the same room. When the experimenter left the room, the model (either a male or a female adult) attacked a doll (commonly known as a "Bobo doll") placed in the room. The model showed various types of aggressive behavior (e.g., hitting it with a mallet, kicking and throwing it) accompanied by verbal aggression (e.g., "Hit him down," "Pow"). After exposure to the aggressive model (or a nonaggressive model in the control condition), children were allowed to play with any of the toys in the room, including the Bobo doll. As shown in Figure 10-2, regardless of the child's own gender and the model's gender, children exposed to the aggressive model behaved more aggressively toward the Bobo doll than children exposed to the nonaggressive model.

Bandura (1965) further demonstrated that imitative aggression, as a learned response, is sensitive to the presence of rewards and punishment. In this experiment, Bandura showed a video of an aggressive adult model to a child. Again, the model attacked the Bobo doll. In one version of the video (the model-rewarded condition), around the end of the video, a second adult appears, praises the behavior, and offers a soft drink and snacks. In the model-punished condition, the second adult says "Hey there, you big bully. You quit picking on that [doll]. I won't tolerate it." The second adult then spanks the model with a rolled-up magazine. In the no consequences condition, the video did not include the second adult. Next, children were allowed to play with the Bobo doll. As shown in Figure 10-3, children in the model-punished condition were the least likely to imitate the model (see the middle dark bars for boys and girls, respectively). After this free play session, however, the researcher told the children "Show me what [the model] did in the TV program" and offered some attractive rewards (e.g., stickers). When imitative aggression was explicitly requested (and incentivized), the differences between conditions disappeared (see the light bars in Figure 10-3). Thus, Bandura concluded that whether socially learned aggression is acted upon is determined at least in part, by anticipated rewards and punishment.

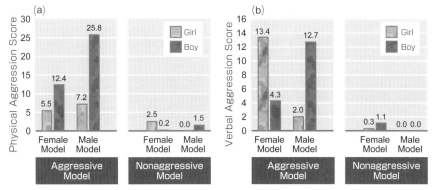

Figure **10**-2. Mean (a) physical and (b) verbal aggression scores as a function of children's gender, the model's gender, and the model's behavior (aggressive vs. nonaggressive). [Bandura et al., 1961 より筆者作成]

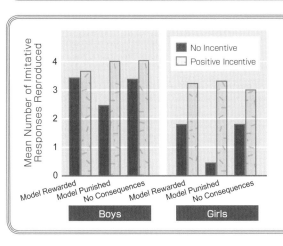

Figure **10**-3. Mean number of imitative aggressive behaviors as a function of children's gender, reinforcement of the model (model rewarded vs. model punished vs. no consequences), and the incentive to imitate (no incentive vs. positive incentive). [Bandura, 1965]

Hostile Aggression：敵意的攻撃

Instrumental Aggression：道具的攻撃

Social Learning Theory：社会的学習理論　　学習理論の要点は，ある行動に対して報酬を受け取るとその行動をとる頻度が高くなり，罰を受けるとその行動をとる頻度が低くなるというものです。社会的学習理論は，自分自身の行動に対する直接的な強化（報酬と罰）がなくても，他者の行動（とそれへの報酬・罰）を観察することでも学習が生じるというものです。

　文献によって，社会学習，観察学習（observational learning），モデリング（modeling），模倣（imitation）など別の表現が用いられていることがあります。

10.3 Obedience to Authority I

One of the worst atrocities in human history is the Holocaust, a large-scale genocide committed by the Nazis during WWII[1]. Not surprisingly, many scholars have aimed to answer the question of why so many Nazi soldiers blindly obeyed orders. Why didn't they revolt? One popular explanation appealed to an internal cause—the **authoritarian personality** of the German people (Adorno, Frenkel-Brunswik, Levinson, & Sanford, 1950). However, in the early 1960s, a social psychologist, Milgram, conducted a social psychological experiment on **obedience to authority**. Quite unexpectedly, he demonstrated that regardless of individual level of authoritarian personality, ordinary people are predisposed to obey orders, even immoral orders, if commanded to do so by an authority figure (Milgram, 1974). The presence of an authority (an external factor) is critical!

Participants in the obedience experiment were men who volunteered to take part in a psychology experiment. When a participant arrived at the laboratory, he met a confederate who was allegedly another participant. The experimenter told the participant and the confederate that the purpose of the experiment was to examine effects of punishment on learning. Next, the participant and the confederate were assigned to the roles of "Teacher" and "Learner," respectively, by an apparently random drawing. The experimenter then explained that the Learner would engage in a memory task (memorizing and recalling pairs of words), and the Teacher (the participant) would give the Learner an electric shock every time the Learner made a mistake.

The shock generator was equipped with many switches, which were associated with different levels of shocks (15 volts to 450 volts in 15-volt increments), accompanied by verbal descriptions, such as "Slight Shock," "Intense Shock" and "XXX." After starting the experiment, the confederate began to (purposely) make mistakes, and the experimenter asked the participant to increase the level of shock after each mistake. As the participant increased the voltage, the confederate made predetermined responses. For example, at 150 volts (Strong Shock), the confederate asked to be released. At 300 volts (Extremely Intense Shock), the confederate screamed in pain and refused to continue answering questions.

Milgram was interested in how ordinary people would respond to immoral orders from an authority figure. If participants requested to stop the experiment, the experimenter gave up to four "prods" to continue (see Table 10-1). If participants requested to stop a fifth time, the experiment was terminated. At what level do you think participants stopped the experiment? Milgram asked this question to some psychologists and psychiatrists before running the experiment. The result of this pre-experimental survey is shown in Figure 10-4. Many experts thought that 150 volts would be the maximum level of shock that ordinary people would be willing to administer.

Table 10-1. Four prods that Milgram (1974) used to encourage the participant to continue the delivery of electric shocks.

Prod 1	Please continue.
Prod 2	The experiment requires that you continue.
Prod 3	It is absolutely essential that you continue.
Prod 4	You have no other choice, you must go on.

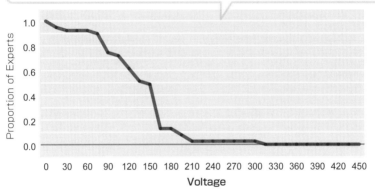

専門家は参加者が与える最大の電気ショック強度を予測するよう求められました。30Vのところで5%ほどグラフが下がっているのは、5%の専門家が参加者は30Vの電気ショックであっても、それをサクラに与えることを拒否すると予測したことを示しています。450Vのところでは0になっていますが、450Vの電気ショックを与える参加者がいると予測した専門家はいなかったということです。

Figure 10-4. The proportion of experts who predicted that participants would deliver each level of shock to the confederate. [Milgram, 1974 より筆者作成]

Authoritarian Personality：権威主義的パーソナリティ（Authoritarianism は「権威主義」）

Obedience（to Authority）：（権威への）服従　ここで紹介している Milgram（1974）の服従実験は、多くのユダヤ人の虐殺に関わったナチスの親衛隊員アドルフ・アイヒマン（Adolf Eichmann）から、日本ではアイヒマン実験と呼ばれることがあります（ただし、英語で Eichmann experiment という表現を使っているのは見たことがありません）。

1　WWII：第二次世界大戦　The Second World War または World War II を省略して WWII と書くので覚えておくとよいでしょう。

10.4 Obedience to Authority II

Were the experts' predictions (Figure 10-4) accurate? The answer is, NO; they were drastically wrong (see Figure 10-5). Unexpectedly to even Milgram himself, the majority of participants increased the voltage all the way to 450 volts (the ends of the dotted and solid lines are above 60%), despite the fact that after 345 volts the Learner stopped responding, as if he had lost consciousness or were dead. These two lines correspond with Milgram's two original conditions: In the *wall pounding condition* (the dotted line), the confederate was placed in a different room, and participants only heard the confederate pounding the wall. In the *wall pounding + shouting condition* (the solid line), participants heard the confederate shouting in the next room as well as his pounding on the wall.

After seeing these results, Milgram made some changes in the experimental setting. Specifically, Milgram brought the confederate into the participant's room, so that participants saw the confederate (who was a professional actor) shouting in pain right next to them. This change reduced the number of participants who gave the 450 volt shock to the confederate. Nevertheless, a substantial portion of participants (16 out of 40 participants) still administered the 450 volt shock (the dashed line in Figure 10-5).

You might suspect that participants did not believe the electric shocks were real. Unfortunately, this was not the case. Many participants took the experiment seriously. Once the confederate started to shout, many participants hesitated to press the button, and asked the experimenter if they could stop the experiment. However, most participants also failed to refuse to continue at least five times (remember that to terminate the experiment, participants had to go through each of the four prods). Participants took the experiment so seriously that some of them even needed clinical intervention after the experiment. For this reason, this experiment stimulated debates about the ethics of psychology experiments. Nowadays, no one can conduct this experiment as it was with Milgram's original design. Ethical committees would stop any researcher who filed a plan for this type of experiment.

However, there is one, rather clever, **replication** study conducted by a psychologist in the 21st century. Burger (2009) noticed that the 150 volt shock was a critical point (see the solid line in Figure 10-5). Once participants passed this point in Milgram's original studies, nearly 80% of participants proceeded to the final 450 volt shock. The 150 volt shock is also important because most experts predicted that participants would never deliver this level of shock (see Figure 10-4). Taking a couple extra precautions (e.g., stopping at 150 volts, immediately debriefing participants), Burger conducted a replication study and found that about 70% of present day American citizens were willing to continue the experiment after the 150 volt shock (see Figure 10-6). The power of authority seems far greater than most of us naïvely (or even professionally) assume.

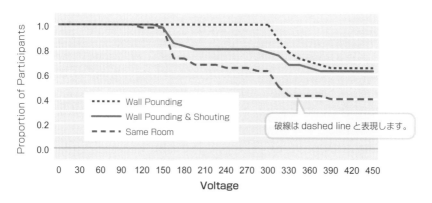

Figure 10-5. The proportion of participants who delivered each level of shock to the confederate as a function of experimental condition. [Milgram, 1974 より筆者作成]

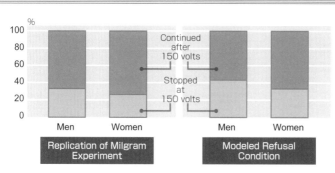

Figure 10-6. The proportion of participants who stopped at 150 volts and continued after 150 volts as a function of gender and the experimental condition. The left-side shows the results of the replication study (with the modifications that Burger made for ethical concerns, and the inclusion of female participants). The right-side shows a new condition (the modeled refusal condition): In this condition, another confederate, who played the role of Teacher, refused to continue the experiment at 90 volts, after which participants took over the confederate's role as Teacher. [Burger, 2009 より筆者作成]

Replication：追試　過去に実施された研究結果が再現されるかどうかを確認するために行われる研究を追試研究といいます。

Advanced Topic: Long-term Effects of Media Violence

When you read the section on social learning theory (Section 10.2), you might have wondered about the effects of exposure to media violence. Young Japanese children are regularly exposed to aggression in TV shows such as Power Rangers,[1] *Kamen Riders*, and *Pretty Cures*. Older children, too, are exposed to entertainment that includes violence (e.g., *Dragon Ball, Naruto, ONE PIECE*). Do children learn aggression from exposure to such media violence? In fact, in the late 20th century, there was a major controversy regarding the long-term influence of exposure to violence (remember that Bandura's studies clearly showed evidence for a short-term influence).

A large body of research finds a *correlation* between childhood exposure to media violence and adulthood aggression. However, critics **doubt** that this correlation implies *causal* influence. For example, aggressive children might be drawn to watch violent TV shows, and become more aggressive adults later on. If this is correct, an aggressive predisposition may yield a *spurious correlation* between childhood exposure to media violence and aggressive behavior in adults. Other possible "third variables" include children's **Socioeconomic Status (SES)**, intelligence, and parenting. Low SES, low intelligence, or poor parenting might increase both childhood exposure to media violence and aggressive behavior in adults.

Although it is nearly impossible to disprove these alternative explanations, the best available evidence indicates that there is a causal effect (Huesmann, Moise-Titus, Podolski, & Eron, 2003). Starting in the 1970s, researchers assessed two **cohorts** of young children (557 first and third graders) in terms of TV violence viewing habits, parent characteristics, and peer impressions of the children's aggressiveness. Approximately twenty years later (in the 1990s), the researchers successfully followed-up with 398 of these individuals, now adults, interviewing both the participants and close others (e.g., spouses, friends).

First, the researchers tested whether levels of childhood aggressiveness would predict adulthood aggression. Among males, it did, whereas among females, it didn't. More importantly, as shown in Figure 10-7, even after statistically controlling for differences in childhood levels of aggression, childhood exposure to TV violence still predicted adulthood aggression! And this was true for both males and females. The researchers next controlled for differences in childhood SES, intelligence, and some parent variables (e.g., parents' aggression). Again, none of these variables were able to erase the significant relationship between childhood exposure to TV violence and adulthood aggression. Of course, these are just correlations, but early exposure to media violence may indeed have an important causal influence on long-term differences in aggression.

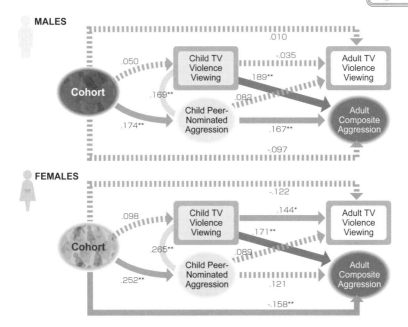

Figure **10**-7. Childhood TV Violence Viewing predicted Adulthood Aggression for both males and females. [Huesmann et al., 2003]

📖 **Doubt と suspect**　辞書を引くと doubt も suspect も「疑う」と書かれていますが，使い方が違います。Doubt は「〜ではない」と疑うのに対して，suspect は「〜だろうと」と疑うのです。
　例えば，「A が B の原因とは思わない」と言いたいときには：
　I doubt that A causes B.（A causes B ではないだろう）
　I suspect that A does not cause B.（A does not cause B だろう）
となります。
　また "I suspect that A causes B." と言うと，「A が B の原因になっているのではないかと疑っている」という意味になります。

Socioeconomic Status（SES）：社会経済的地位（家庭の収入，扶養者の職業，教育などを総合した指標）

Cohort：コホート　調査のときに同じ特徴を共有するグループをコホートといいます。この調査では調査時の年齢で2つのコホートがありました。

1　日本のスーパー戦隊シリーズはアメリカでは Power Rangers シリーズとして知られています。

Supplementary Topic: The Stanford Prison Experiment

Are tyrants made or born? Of course, most people don't consider themselves to be evil. Nevertheless, there is no shortage of tyrannical, "evil" people who exploit others and behave in a sadistic manner. For Phillip Zimbardo, solving the question of evil (i.e., finding out whether evil is the result of inborn personality or more immediate situational influences) was a driving force behind a now notorious behavioral experiment, the **Stanford Prison Experiment**, conducted in the summer of 1971.

Zimbardo set up a mock prison in the basement of the Stanford University Department of Psychology. Of the 24 healthy male university students who volunteered for the two-week experiment, half were randomly assigned to be guards and the other half to be prisoners. To enhance the realism of the experiment, the prisoners were arrested at their homes, and forced to wear prison uniforms upon arrival to the Stanford prison. The guards wore typical prison guard uniforms and mirrored sunglasses.

The first day of the experiment went rather smoothly, but by the second day the inmates started to rebel. For example, they barricaded themselves in their cells, and refused to comply with guards. In response to the rebellion, the guards became increasingly more tyrannical, and abused their prisoners. The guards used push-ups as a common form of punishment, and one of the guards went so far as to step on the prisoners' backs while they were doing these push-ups.

Some of the prisoners had to be released due to apparent mental problems. After the release of one of these prisoners (called #8612), a rumor came to Zimbardo's attention: #8612 was planning on returning to the prison to lead a prison break. Although the prison break never happened, after this rumor the guards became increasingly hostile toward the inmates. They even demanded the prisoners clean toilet bowls with their bare hands.

During the course of the experiment, the prisoners' parents had opportunities to visit their sons. A Catholic priest, who had served as a prison chaplain in real prisons, also visited the mock prison to evaluate the authenticity of the experiment. All of them expressed some concerns. However, it was not until a Stanford psychology graduate student, Christina Maslach, met the guards and prisoners that the experiment was terminated. She strongly opposed the continuation of the experiment as originally scheduled (for two weeks), and thus it ended on the sixth day.

Zimbardo demonstrated how easily people identified with their roles and how strongly these roles (external factors) influence behavior. Some of the otherwise normal university students who were assigned to the guard role became increasingly sadistic and abused their power, while some of those who were assigned to be prisoners had emotional break downs or became extremely submissive to the guards.

Stanford Prison Experiment：スタンフォード監獄実験　　スタンフォード監獄実験では，強い権限を与えられた者が弱い立場の者を虐待してしまうような事態が，いとも簡単に起きてしまうということを示しています。ただし，この実験はどのような要因が虐待を引き起こすかを検討したものではありません。例えば，Zimbardo のイェール大学時代の友人 Gordon Bower は，実験の途中の Zimbardo を訪ねてきたときに，「この実験の独立変数はいったい何だ？」という質問をしたということです。つまり，この実験の学術的な意義は必ずしも自明とはいえないのです。また，後にイギリスの BBC の協力を得て追試実験を行った Reicher & Haslam（2006）は，役割を割り振るだけで簡単に虐待が起きるという解釈に疑問を提起しています。

　その一方，この実験で示されたような虐待は，現実の監獄や捕虜収容所で繰り返し起きています。例えば，2003 年に始まったイラク戦争（アメリカを中心とした国がイラクの武装解除を目的としてイラクへ侵攻した）では，アブグレイブ刑務所においてアメリカ兵から捕虜に対して虐待が行われていたことが明らかになり，関わった軍人が軍法会議にかけられ有罪になっています。日本でも，2001 年から 2002 年にかけて名古屋刑務所の複数の刑務官が，消防用高圧ホースで受刑者に放水し死亡させたり，受刑者の腹部を皮手錠付ベルトで強く締め上げ死亡させるという事件が発生しました。

　もちろん，すべての看守がこのような虐待を行うわけではありません。スタンフォード監獄実験でも穏当な態度をもった看守もいました。しかし，地位の違いと圧倒的な権利の違いが存在する状況は，弱者に対する非人道的な扱いを生みやすい状況であるということは心に留めておく必要があるでしょう。

　下記のサイトでは，Zimbardo が自らの研究を TED カンファレンス[1]で紹介しているビデオを観ることができます。Subtitles から日本語字幕を選ぶこともできます（ただし，虐待の写真などがたくさん出てくるので，視聴の際は注意してください）。
　　http://www.ted.com/talks/philip_zimbardo_on_the_psychology_of_evil
　また Stanford Prison Experiment については，下記のサイトでも要約を読むことができます。
　　http://www.prisonexp.org/

---

[1] TED カンファレンス　　さまざまな分野で影響力のあるアイデアをもつ人たちがプレゼンテーションを行う場。TED（Technology, Entertainment, Design）という団体が開催しています。

References

Adorno, T. W., Frenkel-Brunswik, E., Levinson, D.J., & Sanford, R. N. (1950). *The authoritarian personality*. New York: Norton.

Anderson, C. A., Shibuya, A., Ihori, N., Swing, E. L., Bushman, B. J., Sakamoto, A., Rothstein, H. R., & Saleem, M. (2010). Violent video game effects on aggression, empathy, and prosocial behavior in Eastern and Western countries: A meta-analytic review. *Psychological Bulletin, 136*, 151-173. doi: 10.1037/a0018251

Bandura, A. (1965). Influence of models' reinforcement contingencies on the acquisition of imitative responses. *Journal of Personality and Social Psychology, 1*, 589-595. doi: 10.1037/h0022070

Bandura, A., Ross, D., & Ross, S. A. (1961). Transmission of aggression through imitation of aggressive models. *Journal of Abnormal and Social Psychology, 63*, 575-582. doi: 10.1037/h0045925

Burger, J. M. (2009).Replicating Milgram: Would people still obey today? *American Psychologist, 64*, 1-11. doi: 10.1037/a0010932

Dollard, J., Doob, L. W., Miller, N. E., Mowrer, O. H., & Sears, R. R. (1939). *Frustration and aggression*. New Haven, CT: Yale University Press.

Feshbach, S. (1964). The function of aggression and the regulation of aggressive drive. *Psychological Review, 71*, 257-272. doi: 10.1037/h0043041

Geen, R. G. (1968). Effects of frustration, attack, and prior training in aggressiveness upon aggressive behavior. *Journal of Personality and Social Psychology, 9*, 316-321. doi: 10.1037/h0026054

Hepworth, J. T., & West, S. G. (1988). Lynchings and the economy: A time-series reanalysis of Hovland and Sears (1940). *Journal of Personality and Social Psychology, 55*, 239-247. doi: 10.1037/0022-3514.55.2.239

Hovland, C. I., & Sears, R. R. (1940). Minor studies of aggression: VI. Correlation of lynchings with economic indices. *Journal of Psychology, 9*, 301-310. doi: 10.1080/00223980.1940.9917696

Huesmann, L. R., Moise-Titus, J., Podolski, C.-L., & Eron, L. D. (2003). Longitudinal relations between children's exposure to TV violence and their aggressive and violent behavior in young adulthood: 1977-1992. *Developmental Psychology, 39*, 201-221. doi: 10.1037/0012-1649.39.2.201

Milgram, S. (1974). *Obedience to authority: An experimental view*. New York: Harper & Row. （ミルグラム, S. 山形浩生（訳）(2012).『服従の心理』河出書房新社）

Miller, N. E. (1941). The frustration-aggression hypothesis. *Psychological Review, 48*, 337-342. doi: 10.1037/h0055861

Mintz, A. (1946). A re-examination of correlations between lynchings and economic indices. *Journal of Abnormal and Social Psychology, 41*, 154-160. doi: /10.1037/h0056837

Riecher, S., & Haslam, S. A. (2006). Rethinking the psychology of tyranny: The BBC prison study. *British Journal of Social Psychology, 45*, 1-40. doi: 10.1348/014466605X48998

Wolfgang, M. E. (1958). *Patterns in criminal homicide*. Philadelphia, PA: University of Pennsylvania Press.

Zimbardo, P. (2007). *The Lucifer effect: Understanding how good people turn evil*. New York: Random House.

CHAPTER 11

Cultural Psychology

文化心理学

11.1
How Does Culture Affect the Social Mind?

11.2
Self and Other in the Context of East and West

11.3
Holistic versus Analytic Thought

11.4
Choice and Motivation in the Context of East and West

Advanced Topic
Self and Motivation

11.1 How Does Culture Affect the Social Mind?

This chapter will explore how cultural differences relate to social psychology. We will give special focus to the social psychological processes that differ between East Asian and Western people. We limit our comparisons to these cultures for the following two reasons. First, the majority of research on cross-cultural psychology has compared Eastern and Western populations, and second, this textbook's authors have intuitive access to the cultures of the United States of America (**A.S.**) and Japan (**Y.O.**).

Scholars have long noted that there are some deep differences between the cultures of these two nations. For example, in her 1946 book, *The Chrysanthemum and the Sword*, Benedict claimed that Japan has a **shame culture**, in which one's behaviors are regulated by others' evaluations, whereas America, influenced by Christianity, has a **guilt culture**, in which one's behaviors are regulated by his or her inner conscience. Although the book has been criticized by many scholars, including Japanese scholars, it is still widely read and considered to be a classic in the field of Japanese studies.

Aside from the particular emphasis on Japanese culture, the East-West difference is often characterized by the dimension of **individualism-collectivism** (e.g., Hofstede, Hofstede, & Minkov, 2010; Triandis, 2001). People from collectivistic, Eastern, cultures tend to prioritize their in-group goals more than people from individualistic, Western, cultures. Cultural psychologists often claim that Eastern-Western cultural differences lie rather deeply; they are assumed to affect the very ways we construe our *selves*.

Before beginning, however, it may be fun to take a moment to think about certain untranslatable elements of the Japanese and English languages. Consider the last time you saw one of your friends working hard, studying for a test. What might you have said to your friend in such a situation? In Japanese, it is likely that you said something like 頑張ってね. This literally translates to "Try harder!" or "Work hard!" However, Westerners would never think to say such a thing to a friend who is struggling with studies. Instead, a Westerner would say something like, "Take it easy," "Hang in there,[1]" or even "Don't work too hard!" How is it possible that Japanese and English use such different words in the same situation? As we will learn in the Advanced Topic of this chapter, Westerners see "ability" as more relevant in such situations, while Easterners tend to emphasize "effort." When you tell your Western friend something like "Don't work too hard!" what you are really saying is, "I recognize your ability, and I think you are capable of passing the test." By contrast, Japanese people who hear 頑張ってね, take this message to mean "your effort is important to pass the test." So, the next time you see your American friend working hard, don't say "Work hard!" You may accidentally communicate an unkind message: "I think you lack some relevant ability."

📖 **著者のイニシャル**　論文の中でその論文の著者名がイニシャル（**A. S., Y. O.** など）で表記されていることがままあります。知らない略語が出てきたと思って慌てないでください。

Shame Culture／Guilt Culture：恥の文化／罪の文化　　アメリカの文化人類学者 Ruth Benedict は，その著書 The Chrysanthemum and the Sword（『菊と刀』）で日本とアメリカの文化をこのように表現しました。『菊と刀』は今読んでもとても興味深いので一読をお勧めします。

Individualism-Collectivism：個人主義－集団主義

> **補足9　英語に翻訳しにくい表現**
>
> 　皆さんは友だちがゼミなどで発表を終えたときに「おつかれさま」と言うのではないでしょうか。ためしにインターネットで「おつかれさま／おつかれさまでした」の英語訳がどのようになるか検索してみました。
> 　最初に出てきたのは，"Have a good evening!" や "See you tomorrow" です。職場から帰るときの挨拶としての「おつかれさま」には確かにぴったりです。その日が金曜日であれば，"Thank goodness, it's Friday!" というのも「おつかれさま」に近いと出てきました。
> 　何か共同で仕事をした人に対して別れ際に使うものとして "Nice working with you" という表現，上司が部下にかける言葉として "Thanks for your hard work" という表現も出てきました。どれもゼミの発表を終えた友だちにかける言葉としては不適切ですね。
> 　実はこのような状況でよく使われる表現は "Good job!" や "Great job!" です。直訳すれば「よい発表だったよ」という意味です。皆さんもなるほどと思うかもしれません。ですが，もしかするとアメリカ人と日本人ではまったく違う意味で受けとるかもしれません。アメリカ人は自分の能力が認められたと思うのに，日本人は自分の努力が認められたと思うかもしれません。

1　Hang in There　「最後まであきらめるな」というニュアンスのフレーズで，辞書には「頑張れ」と書いてあることもあります。ただし，このフレーズにも「あなたはやればできるのだから（頑張れ）」という言外の意味があるように思われます。

11.2 Self and Other in the Context of East and West

Cultural psychology rose to prominence in the field of psychology following the publication of Markus and Kitayama's (1991) cornerstone article. They present an extensive review of theoretical discourses and empirical findings documenting the existence of both an Eastern **interdependent** concept of the self (Figure 11-1b), and a Western **independent** concept of the self (Figure 11-1a). The authors conclude that these **cultural self-construals**, in fact, explain a wide array of cultural differences in cognition, emotion, and consequent behavioral styles.

These differences in self-construal translate to different styles of accommodation to each culture. As we already learned, people tend to see the self in a positive light (e.g., Section 2.3). Indeed, many studies conducted in North America have revealed that participants are more sensitive to, and concerned with, information that *enhances* their self-image. This tendency, called **self-enhancement**, was once considered a kernel of human social psychology. However, Markus and Kitayama noticed that studies conducted in Japan not only failed to observe self-enhancement, they showed a diametrically opposite tendency, **self-criticism** (i.e., sensitivity to information that indicates one's weaknesses).

Using a systematic pair of studies, Kitayama and colleagues demonstrated that people in the U.S. and Japan actually differ in terms of self-evaluation styles (Kitayama, Markus, Matsumoto, & Norasakkunkit, 1997). In the first study, both American and Japanese students recalled multiple situations where their self-esteem had either increased or decreased. The researchers then chose 400 representative situations that varied in terms of self-esteem (increased vs. decreased), as well as the participant's country (U.S. vs. Japan) and gender (men vs. women). In the second study, the researchers sampled two different groups of American and Japanese students, and asked whether (i) each situation would be relevant to their self-evaluation if it had happened to them, and if so (ii) how much it would increase or decrease their self-esteem on a 4-point scale (1 = "slightly" to 4 = "very much").

As expected, Japanese students chose a greater number of negative situations as relevant to their self-evaluations, while American students chose a greater number of positive situations. Moreover, on average, Japanese students rated the impact of negative situations as greater than that of positive situations, while American students rated positive situations as more impactful (see Figure 11-2). Self-criticism might appear undesirable (at least if you are from a Western culture). However, according to Kitayama et al. (1997), self-criticism is useful in Japan because knowing one's own weaknesses helps one to "meet the standards of excellence shared in a given social unit" (p. 1246).

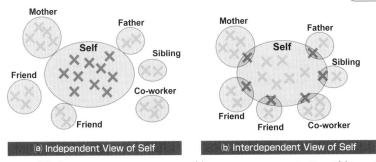

Figure 11-1. Two cultural self-construals: (a) Independent view of self and (b) interdependent view of self. [Markus & Kitayama, 1991]

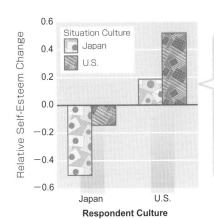

図の Situation Culture は，日本人とアメリカ人のいずれが報告した状況を刺激として用いたかを示しています。この研究では，アメリカで学ぶ日本人留学生にも同じ調査が実施されました。その結果，日本人とアメリカ人の中間の（ややアメリカナイズされた）結果が得られました。ただし，この結果だけからは，留学したことでアメリカナイズされたのか，そもそもそういうタイプの人が留学しがちだったのかはわかりません。

Figure 11-2. Relative self-esteem change (the average expected impact of positive situations minus the average expected impact of negative situations) as a function of the origin of participants and the origin of situations. [Kitayama et al., 1997]

Cultural Self-Construal：文化的自己観　Construal は，理解するという意味の construe の名詞で，self-construal は自己についての理解という意味で自己観といいます。

　自己とは他者と切り離されたものであるという**相互独立的自己観**（**independent self-construal**）が優勢な西洋では，人々には**自己高揚**（**self-enhancement**）傾向があります。一方，自己とは他者との関係性にわかちがたくむすびついているという**相互協調的自己観**（**interdependent self-construal**）が優勢な東洋では，**自己批判**（**self-criticism**）傾向が見られます。

11.3 Holistic versus Analytic Thought

A common English idiom asks "Can you see the forest for the trees?" If your answer to this question is YES, this means you tend to focus on the whole picture (i.e., the entire forest), and you are likely from an interdependent culture such as Japan. If your answer is NO, this means you tend to analyze focal details (i.e., an individual tree), and you are likely from an independent culture such as America. The historical antecedents that have led to this cultural difference are vast and beyond the scope of this section, but put simply, it appears that East Asians tend to see wholes (**holistic** attention), whereas Westerners tend to see parts (**analytic** attention). In other words, it is expected that even when they are exposed to the same scene, East Asians pay more attention to contextual (or background) information, while Westerners pay more attention to the focal object.

Masuda and Nisbett (2001) conducted the original empirical study to verify this claim. Participants were initially informed that they would be observing a series of animated scenes about which they would later be asked some questions. They were then briefly presented with scenes that depicted a lively underwater environment (see Figure 11-3). The focal items in the scene were a few large fish that moved from one side of the scene to the other. In the background were a number of other items, including small fish, frogs, snails, various plants, bubbles, and other miscellaneous objects. As the key dependent variable, participants described what they saw in the animations. As expected, Japanese participants mentioned background items more frequently than American participants. Moreover, when the researchers analyzed participants' very first response, American participants mentioned the focal objects more frequently, whereas Japanese participants mentioned the background objects more frequently (see Figure 11-4).

Masuda and Nisbett further tested their hypothesis in an ingenious manner. If East Asians see a particular object in relation to the background, they are likely to be confused if the object is embedded in a novel background. Therefore, after the free-recall session, Masuda and Nisbett presented pictures of fish (some from the animations and others that were new), and asked if participants saw each fish in the animations. In this test, the fish were displayed with either the original background, no background, or a novel background. As expected, when objects from the scene were presented in a novel context (i.e., in front of a new background), the memory performance of Japanese participants was negatively affected. On the other hand, American participants' recognition was not significantly affected by background information (see Figure 11-5). This study provides empirical evidence that Japanese people tend to process information from a complex visual scene in a more "holistic" manner, while American people tend to see the same scene more "analytically," detaching individual objects from contextual information.

Figure 11-3. An example scene from Masuda and Nisbett's (2001) animations.［作成者（増田貴彦）の許可を得て掲載］

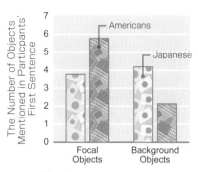

Figure 11-4. Mean number of objects (focal vs. background) mentioned in participants' first sentence as a function of their nationality.［Masuda & Nisbett, 2001 より筆者作成］

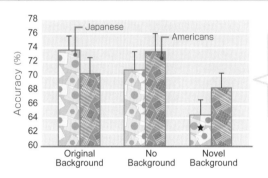

Figure 11-5. Accuracy of recall of Japanese and American participants as a function of background.［Masuda & Nisbett, 2001］

日本人では魚の絵が元の背景とは違う（新しい）背景とともに提示されたときに判断の正確さが有意に下がりました（★で示しています。）一方，アメリカ人の判断の正確さは背景には影響されませんでした。

Holistic Thought／Analytic Thought：包括的思考／分析的思考　説明対象となる事象を文脈から切り離し，その事象そのものの特性などからものごとを説明しようとする思考スタイルを分析的思考といいます。一方，その事象をとりまく文脈や「場」にも注意を払い，その事象と文脈との関係からものごとを説明しようとする思考方法を包括的思考といいます。

　前者は古代ギリシア以来の知的伝統にその起源をもち，後者は儒教や道教の影響を受けていると考えられています。

11.4 Choice and Motivation in the Context of East and West

People want to control their lives, not have things pressed upon them. This sounds like a truism, and traditional research on **intrinsic motivation** has confirmed the validity of this idea. Participants are more motivated to perform a task when they choose, by themselves, to engage in the task. However, some researchers questioned whether this is *universally* true. Consider the following excerpt from Iyengar and Lepper's (1999) article (p. 350):

> John goes out to dinner with friends. As he peruses the menu, he spots a favorite dish... To his dismay, however, he listens as the two companions sitting across from him order this same item. Suddenly, he faces a "dilemma of individuality" and must decide whether to go ahead and order the same dish... Even if he resists the temptation to change his planned order, he may still find himself obliged to offer some prefatory apology or explanation for his decision: "I hate to be such a copycat" or "I was really planning on ordering that dish all along."

We bet most of you do not share John's dilemma. You are probably happy to see that your friends enjoy the same food as you. Perhaps you even feel it is easier, less stressful, if everyone just orders the same dish.

This is likely because you (as an East Asian) value group harmony more than personal choice. Iyengar and Lepper tested this intuitive notion by conducting an innovative study. Studies before them tended only to compare a personal choice condition, where participants themselves choose what task they perform, and a no-choice condition, where the experimenter chooses the task for the participants. The typical result observed in America was that participants perform better on an experimental task in a personal choice condition than in a no-choice condition. But what happens when the task is chosen by a member of one's ingroup? To test this, the researchers added the so-called, "mom choice" condition, where the mothers of participants (7-9 year old schoolchildren) made the choice of task for them.

European American children showed the traditional pattern: They performed the task (i.e., solving anagrams[1]) better and engaged in it longer during the free-play session, when they chose the task by themselves than when the experimenter or their mother chose it for them (Figures 11-6 and 11-7). On the other hand, Asian American children performed better and engaged in the task longer when their mother chose it for them than when they made the choice by themselves. Iyengar and Lepper conducted a second study where their friend, instead of their mother, made the choice for them. Again, the results showed the same pattern. Asian American children are more motivated when their significant other (their mother or friend) makes a choice for them. These results clearly show that the apparent truism about choice and motivation (i.e., that people like to choose for themselves) needs some qualification.

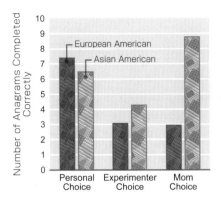

Figure 11-6. Mean number of anagrams correctly completed by European American children and Asian American children as a function of choice condition. [Iyengar & Lepper, 1999]

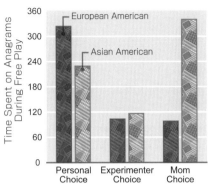

Figure 11-7 Mean time (in seconds) spent on anagrams during a free-play period as a function of choice condition. [Iyengar & Lepper, 1999]

Intrinsic Motivation：**内発的動機づけ**　　作業それ自体が面白いからそれをするといったような，その個人の内側から出てくる動機のことです。これに対して，報酬など作業をする理由が外から与えられる場合は，外発的動機づけといいます。

1　Anagram：アナグラム　　ある単語に含まれるアルファベットを並べ替えて別の意味の言葉にする遊びのことです。例えば，choice という単語に含まれるアルファベット（c, h, o, i, c, e）を並べ替えると，echoic になります。

Advanced Topic: Self and Motivation

Imagine you received a test result that indicates your score is below the average of your classmates. If you are like Japanese participants in Heine et al.'s (2001) experiment, you may think "I have to put forth more effort to master the subject." If this sounds natural to you, that's because you hold an **incremental theory** of self. You likely believe the self is changeable, and that your achievement depends on your effort. Nonetheless, this is hardly a universal view. In Western countries, people tend to hold an **entity theory** of self. According to this view, the self is characterized by relatively fixed, unchangeable attributes.

Heine et al. predicted that these culturally dominant views of self may lead people in different cultures to react to their successes/failures in different ways. People from Eastern countries (who hold the incremental theory) may feel like they have to try harder after experiencing failures: "I can do better!" On the other hand, people from Western countries (who hold the entity theory) may feel motivated to try harder after experiencing a success: "I must cultivate my natural talent!"

In Heine et al.'s experiment, participants first engaged in a set of puzzles, purportedly measuring creativity. After the task, half of the participants were told that their score was well above average among their fellow university students (the success condition). The other half were told that their score was well below average (the failure condition). Next, the experimenter pretended the computer had suddenly broken, and rushed to a professor's office to resolve the problem. The experimenter explained to the participant that because it could take some time until the experiment would be fixed, the participant may want to work on another set of puzzles. After leaving the room, the experimenter entered an adjoining room and secretly timed how long participants kept working on the puzzles.

As shown in Figure 11-8, Japanese participants persisted much longer in the failure condition than in the success condition. They apparently tried to mend their weakness. Canadian students, however, persisted longer in the success condition. The newfound knowledge of their talent evidently served as a motivation to continue.

In a subsequent experiment, Heine et al. showed that the cultural effect of failure can be altered by explicitly telling participants about the role of effort in the task (Heine et al., 2001, Study 3). As shown in Figure 11-9, when American participants were told that their performance depends on effort, they became more persistent: "My previous failure was not a reflection of my true ability." By contrast, when Japanese were told that effort would likely *not* improve their performance, Japanese students became less persistent: "If I can't change, why try?" This research clearly indicates that implicit theories about the self have real effects on motivation.

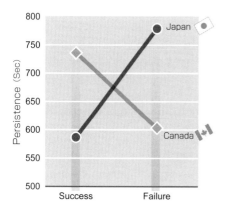 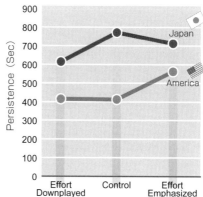

Figure 11-8 Persistence time (in seconds) of Japanese and Canadian participants after success and failure feedback. [Heine et all., 2001]

Figure 11-9 Persistence time (in seconds) of Japanese and American participants after failure feedback as a function of effort condition—the role of effort is downplayed (left) or emphasized (right). [Heine et all., 2001]

Incremental Theory/Entity Theory：拡大理論／実体理論　これらの用語は，動機づけ研究者の Carol Dweck の説に基づいています。これらはいずれも「理論」といっていますが，学術的な意味での理論ではありません。ここでは，素朴理論（誰もが素朴に理解している内容）という意味で使われているので注意してください。

References

Benedict, R. (1946). *The chrysanthemum and the sword: Patterns of Japanese culture*. Boston, Houghton Mifflin.（日本語版は『菊と刀』というタイトルで3種類の翻訳〔長谷川松治訳，角田安正訳，越智敏之・越智道雄訳〕が出版されています）

Heine, S. J., Kitayama, S., Lehman, D. R., Takata, T., Ide, E., Leung, C., & Matsumoto, H. (2001). Divergent consequences of success and failure in Japan and North America: An investigation of self-improving motivations and malleable selves. *Journal of Personality and Social Psychology, 81*, 599-615. doi: 10.1037/0022-3514.81.4.599

Hofstede, G., Hofstede, G. J., & Minkov, M. (2010). *Cultures and organizations: Software of the mind* (3rd ed.). New York: McGraw-Hill.（ホフステード，G.，ホフステード，G. J.，& ミンコフ，M. 岩井八郎・岩井紀子（訳）(2013).『多文化世界——違いを学び未来への道を探る』（原著第3版）有斐閣）

Iyengar, S. S., & Lepper, M. R. (1999). Rethinking the value of choice: A cultural perspective on intrinsic motivation. *Journal of Personality and Social Psychology, 76*, 349-366. doi:10.1037/0022-3514.76.3.349

Kitayama, S., Markus, H. R., Matsumoto, H., & Norasakkunkit, V. (1997). Individual and collective processes in the construction of the self: Self-enhancement in the United States and self-criticism in Japan. *Journal of Personality and Social Psychology, 72*, 1245-1267. doi: 10.1037/0022-3514.72.6.1245

Markus, H. R., & Kitayama, S. (1991). Culture and the self: Implications for cognition, emotion, and motivation. *Psychological Review, 98*, 224-253. doi: 10.1037/0033-295X.98.2.224

Masuda, T., & Nisbett, R. E. (2001). Attending holistically versus analytically: Comparing the context sensitivity of Japanese and Americans. *Journal of Personality and Social Psychology, 81*, 922-934. doi: 10.1037/0022-3514.81.5.922

Triandis, H. C. (2001). Individualism-collectivism and personality. *Journal of Personality, 69*, 907-924. doi: 10.1111/1467-6494.696169

Index
索　引

人名索引

Abrahams, D. 52
Ackerman, P. 110
Adorno, T. W. 124
Ajzen, I. 68
Al Ramiah, A. 103
Allport, F. H. 69, 80, 81
Allport, G. W. 68, 69, 81, 102
Amsterdam, B. 16
Anderson, N. H. 46
Arnold, M. B. 62
Aron, A. P. 60, 61
Aronson, E. 70, 71, 74
Aronson, V. 52
Asch, S. E. 44-46, 84-87
Back, K. 48
Backman, C. W. 50
Banaji, M. R. 104
Bandura, A. 122, 123, 128
Batson, C. D. 108-111
Baumeister, R. F. 24, 90
Benedict, R. 134, 135
Billig, M. G. 98
Birch, K. 110
Bond, C. F., Jr. 81
Bornstein, R. F. 48
Bower, G. H. 56, 57
Brown, J. D. 20, 21
Buckley, T. 110
Bundy, R. P. 98
Burger, J. M. 126, 127
Byrne, D. 50, 51
Cacioppo, J. T. 74
Cannon, W. 60
Cantril, H. 100, 101
Carlsmith, J. M. 70, 71, 74
Carlston, D. E. 46, 47
Carpenter, M. 115
Cheung, C. K. T. 90

Choi, W. 90
Cialdini, R. B. 72, 73, 98, 99
Cohen, C. E. 34, 35
Cooley, C. H. 16
D'Agostino, P. R. 48
Darley, J. M. 108, 109, 112-115
Davison, L. 62
Deutsch, M. 86, 87
Dollard, J. 120, 121
Doob, L. W. 120
Downs, D. L. 24
Duncan, B. D. 110
Dutton, G. D. 60, 61
Dweck, C. 143
Eisenberger, N. I. 90
Ekman, P. 64, 65
Elliott, J. 94, 95
Ellis, B. 52
Eron, L. D. 128
Fehr, E. 116
Feshbach, S. 122
Festinger, L. 22, 23, 31, 48, 49, 70
Fishbein, M. 68
Flament, C. 98
Fraser, S. C. 72, 73
Freedman, J. L. 72, 73
Frenkel-Brunswik, E. 124
Friesen, W. V. 64, 65
Gächter, S. 116
Gallup, G. G., Jr. 16, 17
Gansberg, M. 112
Geen, R. G. 120
Gerard, H. B. 86, 87
Gifford, R. K. 36, 37
Goldman, R. 74
Greene, D. 40
Greenwald, A. G. 76, 77
Hamilton, D. L. 36, 37

145

Hamilton, T. E. 53
Harkins, S. 82
Harris, V. A. 32, 33
Haslam, S. A. 131
Hastorf, A. H. 100, 101
Heider, F. 32, 33
Heine, S. J. 142, 143
Hepworth, J. T. 121
Hewstone, M. 103
Hofstede, G. 134
Hofstede, G. J. 134
House, P. 40
Hovland, C. I. 120, 121
Huesmann, L. R. 128, 129
Iyengar, S. S. 140, 141
James, W. 16, 17, 58
Jones, E. E. 32, 33
Kahneman, D. 38, 39
Kalick, S. M. 53
Keizer, K. 4–6, 8
Kelley, H. H. 44, 52
Kitayama, S. 136, 137
Kubota, J. T. 104
Kuhn, M. H. 16
Kunda, Z. 30, 31, 40–42
Lage, E. 88
Lange, C. 58
LaPiere, R. T. 68
Latané, B. 82, 83, 86, 87, 112–115
Lazarus, R. S. 62, 63
Leary, M. R. 24, 25
LeDoux, J. 63
Lepper, M. R. 140, 141
Levinson, D. J. 124
Lichtman, R. R. 22
Lieberman, M. D. 90
Lindenberg, S. 4
Markus, H. R. 18, 19, 136, 137
Martin, L. L. 58
Masuda, T. 138, 139
Matsumoto, H. 136
McGhee, D. E. 76
McPartland, T. S. 16
Milgram, S. 124–127

Miller, N. E. 120, 121
Minkov, M. 134
Mintz, A. 121
Mischel, W. 26, 27
Moise-Titus, J. 128
Mordkoff, A. 62
Moscovici, S. 88, 89
Mowrer, O. H. 120
Naffrechoux, M. 88
Nelson, D. 50, 51
Nemeth, C. J. 88
Newman, L. S. 68, 69
Nisbett, R. E. 10, 11, 40–42, 138, 139
Norasakkunkit, V. 136
Over, H. 115
Park, B. 100, 101
Payne, B. K. 104, 105
Pettigrew, T. F. 102, 103
Petty, R. E. 74, 75
Phelps, E. A. 104, 105
Plötner, M. 115
Podolski, C.-L. 128
Riecher, S. 131
Rodin, J. 114
Rodriguez, M. L. 26
Rose, T. L. 36
Ross, D. 122
Ross, L. 40
Ross, S. A. 122
Rothbart, M. 100, 101
Rottman, L. 52
Sanford, R. N. 124
Schachter, S. 48, 60
Schwartz, J. L. K. 76
Sears, R. R. 120, 121
Secord, P. F. 50
Sedikides, C. 23
Sherif, M. 96, 97
Shoda, Y. 26
Shotland, R. L. 113
Simpson, B. 12, 13
Singer, J. 60
Skowronski, J. J. 46, 47
Speisman, J. C. 62, 63

Steg, L.	4	Tversky, A.	38, 39
Steiner, I. D.	82, 83	Van Lange, P. A. M.	12
Stepper, S.	58	Walster, E.	52, 53
Strack, F.	58, 59	Weigel, R. H.	68, 69
Straw, M. K.	113	West, S. G.	121
Strube, M. J.	23	Wicker, A. W.	68
Tajfel, H.	98, 99	Willer, R.	12, 13
Tambor, E. S.	24	Williams, K. D.	82, 90, 91
Taylor, S. E.	20–22	Wills, T. A.	22
Terdal, S. K.	24	Wilson, T. D.	10, 11
Titus, L. J.	81	Wolfgang, M. E.	120
Tomasello, M.	115	Wood, J. B.	22
Triandis, H. C.	134	Yamagishi, T.	116, 117
Triplett, N.	80, 81	Zajonc, R. B.	48, 49, 62, 63, 80
Tropp, L. R.	102, 103	Zimbardo, P.	130, 131
Turner, J.	74, 98		

英語事項索引

affect　56, 57
aggression　120–123, 128, 129
aggressive behavior　120, 122, 123, 128
altruism　108–110
altruistic behavior　109, 110
altruistic punishment　116, 117
amygdala　104, 105
analytic thought, analytic attention　138, 139
anchoring and adjustment heuristic　38, 39
antisocial behavior　2, 4, 6, 8, 120
attitude　68, 69, 76, 77
attitude-behavior relationship　68–70
attribution theory　33
authoritarian personality　124, 125
availability heuristic　38, 39
base rate fallacy　38, 39
basic emotions　64, 65
basking in reflected glory　98, 99
BIRGing　⇒ basking in reflected glory
Broken Window Theory　4–6, 8
bystander effect　114, 115
Cannon-Bard theory　60, 61
causal relationship, causal influence　6–8, 128

central trait　44, 45
co-action　80, 81
cognitive appraisal theory　62, 63
cognitive bias　30, 38–40, 100
cognitive dissonance theory　70, 71
collectivism　134, 135
confederate　84–86, 108–110, 124–127
conformity　84–86, 88
conjunction fallacy　38, 39
construct　6, 7
contact hypothesis, contact theory　102, 103
(experimental) control　8, 9
cooperation　116, 117
coordination loss　82, 83
CORFing　⇒ cutting off reflected failure
correlation　7, 128
correspondence bias　32, 33
cultural self-construal　136, 137
cutting off reflected failure　99
Cyberball　90, 91
debriefing　95
deception　50, 51
delay of gratification　26, 27

dependent variable 8, 9	informational influence 86, 87
diffusion of responsibility 82, 83, 114, 115	ingroup 96–98, 100, 120, 140
discrimination 94, 95	ingroup favoritism 98, 99, 102
disposition 4, 5, 12	instrumental aggression 122, 123
door-in-the-face technique 72, 73	interaction effect 12, 13
downward social comparison 22, 23	interdependent self-construal 137
dual process model of persuasion 74, 75	intergroup conflict 96, 98
effect size 102, 103	intergroup contact theory ⇒ contact hypothesis
elaboration likelihood model 75	internal attribution 32, 33
emotion 56, 57	internal factor 32, 33
empathy 110	interpersonal attraction 50
empathy-altruism hypothesis 110, 111	intrinsic motivation 140, 141
entity theory 142, 143	introspection 10, 11
external attribution 32, 33	I-self 16, 58
external factor 2, 3, 32, 33, 108, 112, 120, 124, 130	James-Lange theory 58–60
false consensus effect 40, 41	(response) latency 18, 19, 76, 105
field experiment 8, 9, 96	looking-glass self 16, 17
fMRI ⇒ functional magnetic resonance imaging	main effect 13
foot-in-the-door technique 72, 73	(experimental) manipulation 8, 9
free-ride, free-load 82, 83, 116, 117	marshmallow test 26, 27
free-rider problem 116, 117	matching hypothesis 52, 53
frustration-aggression hypothesis 120, 121	media violence 128
functional magnetic resonance imaging 90, 91	(statistical) mediation 103
fundamental attribution error 32, 33	mere exposure effect 48, 49, 62
gambler's fallacy 38, 39	me-self 16, 18, 58
guilt culture 134, 135	meta-analysis 81, 102, 103
halo effect 10, 11	minimal group paradigm 98, 99
helping behavior 108, 110, 112–114	minority influence 88, 89
heuristic(s) 38, 39	mirror test 16, 17
heuristic-systematic model 75	misattribution 60, 61
holistic thought, holistic attention 138, 139	modern racism 105
hostile aggression 122, 123	mood 56, 57
hypothalamus 60, 61	mood congruence effect 56, 57
hypothesis 4–6	motivation loss 82, 83
IAT ⇒ implicit association test	need to belong 90, 91
illusion of control 20, 21	negativity bias 46, 47
illusory correlation 36, 37	normative influence 86, 87
implicit association test 76, 77, 104	obedience (to authority) 124, 125
impression formation 44–46	operational definition 6, 7
incremental theory 142, 143	ostracism ⇒ social exclusion
independent self-construal 137	outgroup 96, 97, 100
independent variable 8, 9	outgroup homogeneity effect, outgroup homogeneity bias 100, 101
individualism 134, 135	
information integration theory 46, 47	(experimental) participant 8, 9

peripheral trait　　44, 45
person-situation interaction　　12, 13
persuasion　　72, 74
physical attractiveness　　52, 53
physiological arousal　　60-62
positive illusions　　20-22, 24, 56
prejudice　　76, 94, 95, 102, 103
propinquity　　⇒ proximity
prosocial behavior　　2, 13, 108-110, 116
proximity (as an antecedent of interpersonal attraction)　　48, 49
public good　　116, 117
punishment　　⇒ altruistic punishment
random assignment　　8, 9, 24
reaction time　　⇒ response time
realistic conflict theory　　96, 97
reciprocal liking, reciprocity of liking　　50, 51
replication　　126, 127
representativeness heuristic　　38, 39
response time　　18, 19
Robbers Cave Experiment　　96, 97, 102
sanction system　　116, 117
schadenfreude　　22, 23
schema　　18, 19
self　　16, 17, 136, 142
self-assessment　　22, 23
self-criticism　　136, 137
self-enhancement　　23, 24, 136, 137
self-esteem　　24, 25, 90, 98, 136, 137
self-evaluation　　20, 22, 23, 136
self-regulation　　16, 26, 27
self-schema　　18, 19
self-serving bias　　30, 31
self-verification　　23
SES　　⇒ socioeconomic status

shame culture　　134, 135
similarity (as an antecedent of interpersonal attraction)　　50-52
situational factor　　2-4
situational influence　　4, 12, 108, 130
social cognition　　20, 30, 31, 40, 100
social comparison　　22, 23
social exclusion　　90, 91
social facilitation　　80-82
social identity　　98, 99
social impact theory　　86, 87
social influence　　86, 87
social inhibition　　81
social learning theory　　122, 123, 128
social loafing　　82, 83, 114
social value orientation　　12, 13
socioeconomic status　　128, 129
sociometer theory　　24, 25
source credibility　　74, 75
spurious (correlation)　　120, 121, 128
Stanford Prison Experiment　　130, 131
state self-esteem　　25
stereotype　　34-36
stooge　　⇒ confederate
subject　　⇒ participant
superordinate goal　　96, 97
symbolic racism　　104, 105
thalamus　　60, 61
The Chrysanthemum and the Sword　　134, 135
theory　　6, 7
third-party punishment　　⇒ altruistic punishment
trait self-esteem　　25
twenty statements test　　16, 17
two-factor theory of emotion　　60-63
upward social comparison　　22, 23

日本語事項索引

あ 行

誤った合意性推論　　⇒フォールス・コンセンサス効果

因果関係　　7
印象形成　　45
栄光浴　　99
fMRI　　⇒機能的磁気共鳴画像法

オストラシズム　⇒社会的排除，社会的排斥

か 行

外集団　97, 101, 103
外集団等質性効果　101
外的帰属　33
外的要因　3, 33
外発的動機づけ　141
拡大理論　143
仮説　5
下方比較　23
感情　57
『菊と刀』　135
擬似相関　121
基準率無視　39
帰属理論　33
機能的磁気共鳴画像法（fMRI）　91
規範的影響　87
気分　57
気分一致効果　57
基本感情　⇒基本情動
基本情動　65
基本的帰属のエラー　33
客我　17
キャノン=バード説　61
ギャンブラーの錯誤　39
鏡映的自己　17
共感　111
共感・利他性仮説　111
協力　117
近接性　49
傾性　5
係留と調整のヒューリスティック　39
権威主義的パーソナリティ　125
顕在態度　77
現実的葛藤理論　97, 99
現代的人種差別主義　105
好意の返報性　51
効果量　103
公共財　117
攻撃　121, 123
交互作用効果　13
向社会的行動　13, 109
構成概念　7

誤帰属　61
個人主義　135
コントロール幻想　21

さ 行

最小条件集団パラダイム　99
サイバーボール課題　91
錯誤相関　37
（実験の）サクラ　85
差別　95, 99
サマーキャンプ実験　⇒泥棒洞窟実験
（実験）参加者　9
ジェームズ=ランゲ説　59
自己　17
自己確証動機　23
自己高揚　23, 137
自己高揚動機　23
自己査定動機　23
自己スキーマ　19
自己制御　27
自己批判　137
自己評価　23
自己奉仕バイアス　31
視床　61
視床下部　61
自尊感情　25
実験操作　⇒操作
実体理論　143
社会経済的地位　129
社会的アイデンティティ　99
社会的インパクト理論　87
社会的影響　87
社会的学習理論　123
社会的価値志向性　13
社会的促進　81
社会的手抜き　83
社会的認知　31
社会的排除，社会的排斥　91
社会的比較　23
社会的抑制　81
シャーデンフロイデ　23
従属変数　9
集団間葛藤　97
集団主義　135

周辺特性　45
主　我　17
主効果　13
順社会的行動　⇒向社会的行動
上位目標　97
状況要因　3, 13
状態自尊感情　25
象徴的人種差別主義　105
情　動　57
情動の二要因理論　61
情報的影響　87
情報統合理論　47
上方比較　23
所属欲求　91
身体的魅力度　53
スキーマ　19
スクリプト　19
スタンフォード監獄実験　131
ステレオタイプ　35, 95
制裁システム　117
精緻化見込みモデル　75
生理的覚醒　61
生理的喚起　⇒生理的覚醒
責任の分散　83, 115
接触仮説　103
説　得　73
説得の二重過程モデル　75
潜在態度　77
潜在連合テスト　77
相関関係　7
相互協調的自己観　137
相互独立的自己観　137
（実験）操作　9
操作の定義　7
ソシオメーター理論　25

た 行

対応バイアス　33
第三者罰　117
態　度　69, 77
代表性ヒューリスティック　39
ただ乗り　83, 117
ただ乗り問題　117
単純接触効果　49

中心特性　45
調整の失敗　83
追　試　127
つり合い仮説　53
ディセプション　51
敵意的攻撃　123
デブリーフィング　95
ドア・イン・ザ・フェース・テクニック　73
動機づけの低下　83
道具的攻撃　123
統　制　9
同　調　85
特性自尊感情　25
独立変数　9
泥棒洞窟実験　97

な 行

内　観　11
内集団　97, 101
内集団ひいき　99
内　省　11
内的帰属　33
内的要因　33
内発的動機づけ　141
20答法　17
認知的評価理論　63
認知的不協和理論　71
認知バイアス　39
ネガティヴィティ・バイアス　47

は 行

（統計的）媒介　103
恥の文化／罪の文化　135
罰　117
ハロー効果　11
反社会的行動　5
反応時間　19
反応潜時　19
被験者　⇒参加者
人と状況のインタラクション　13
ヒューリスティック（ス）　39
ヒューリスティック・システマティックモデル　75
フィールド実験　9

フォールス・コンセンサス効果　41
（権威への）服従　125
フット・イン・ザ・ドア・テクニック　73
フラストレーション・攻撃仮説　121
文化的自己観　137
分析的思考　139
偏　見　95, 99, 103
扁桃核（扁桃体）　105
包括的思考　139
傍観者効果　115
ポジティヴ・イリュージョン　21

　　ま 行

マシュマロ・テスト　27
満足の遅延　27

ミラーテスト　17
無作為割りつけ　⇒ランダム・アサインメント
メタ分析　81, 103

　　ら 行

ランダム・アサインメント　9
利他主義, 利他性　109, 111
利他的罰　117
利用可能性ヒューリスティック　39
理　論　7
類似性　51
連言錯誤　39

　　わ 行

割れ窓理論　5, 9

英語で学ぶ社会心理学
Learning Social Psychology in English

〈有斐閣ブックス〉

2017年12月25日　初版第1刷発行
2025年 1 月25日　初版第6刷発行

著　者　　大　坪　庸　介
　　　　　アダム・スミス

発行者　　江　草　貞　治

発行所　　株式会社　有　斐　閣

郵便番号 101-0051
東京都千代田区神田神保町 2-17
https://www.yuhikaku.co.jp/

印刷　大日本法令印刷株式会社／製本　牧製本印刷株式会社
文字情報処理・レイアウト　田中あゆみ
© 2017, Yohsuke OHTSUBO, Adam SMITH. Printed in Japan
落丁・乱丁本はお取替えいたします。
★定価はカバーに表示してあります。
ISBN 978-4-641-18436-7

JCOPY　本書の無断複写(コピー)は、著作権法上での例外を除き、禁じられています。複写される場合は、そのつど事前に(一社)出版者著作権管理機構(電話03-5244-5088, FAX03-5244-5089, e-mail：info@jcopy.or.jp)の許諾を得てください。